THE
MOUNT
WASHINGTON
TRANSIT TUNNEL
DISASTER

THE
MOUNT
WASHINGTON
TRANSIT TUNNEL
DISASTER

MARY JANE KUFFNER HIRT

THE
History
PRESS

Published by The History Press
Charleston, SC
www.historypress.com

First published 2021

Manufactured in the United States

ISBN 9781467142717

Library of Congress Control Number: 2021934134

Notice: The information in this book is true and complete to the best of our knowledge. It is offered without guarantee on the part of the author or The History Press. The author and The History Press disclaim all liability in connection with the use of this book.

To everyone over the years who found the Knoxville #4236 trolley accident story compelling and encouraged me to pursue this project.
My sincere thanks to all.

CONTENTS

PREFACE

This story about the December 24, 1917 Mount Washington Transit Tunnel disaster grew out of an effort to solve a family mystery. About a dozen years ago, my mother told me that my Grandpa Kuffner's cousin had died in a trolley accident in Pittsburgh. Although she thought it happened in the early 1900s, she didn't know the cousin's name, gender or age. After several visits to Carnegie Library to read newspaper microfilms, I concluded that in the early 1900s, incidents involving streetcars, horses and wagons, pedestrians and/or motor vehicles causing death or injury were quite common. I also decided it was unlikely that I would ever determine who the cousin was or learn anything about the accident. That all changed, though, a few years later when my mother found a critical clue in the *Pittsburgh Post-Gazette*'s almanac for December 24, 2011:

> *1917 Twenty people were killed in a Mount Washington streetcar accident in one of Pittsburgh's worst transit tragedies.*

Early on December 26, 2011, I went back to Carnegie Library to read newspaper microfilms. The first local news accounts of the accident were horrific. More than 120 passengers crowded onto the trolley at the south end of the tunnel; 18 died immediately when the car overturned as it exited the North Portal of the Mount Washington Tunnel at West Carson and Smithfield Streets. The loss and its aftermath would over shadow the city and its neighboring communities for months, if not years.

Reprint from *Pittsburgh Post-Gazette*, December 31, 2017.

After reading through the list of dead and injured, I searched for obituaries to see whether Grandpa's cousin was one of the twenty-three who ultimately died. The first name on the list published by the *Pittsburgh Post*, Mrs. Leo Czerny, was my grandpa's cousin. Her obituary gave her maiden name as Kuffner. Aurelia Kuffner Czerny, age forty-five, the mother of seven children, lived at 438 Althea Street in Beltzhoover. Leopold Czerny, age forty-eight, her husband, was also seriously injured in the accident.

Little did I know, until finding Leopold Czerny's citizenship petition, that Irene Czerny Walenta, a woman my family had visited decades before, was one of Aurelia's seven children. The Czerny family had immigrated to Pittsburgh from Austria-Hungary in the fall of 1909 and became naturalized American citizens in September 1915.

Finding the almanac entry turned from accidental to serendipitous when I later discovered that in the fourteen years the *Pittsburgh Post-Gazette* had published an almanac on December 24, the paper's first mention of the Mount Washington Tunnel accident appeared on December 24, 2011.

My intent in writing this book was to establish a cohesive historical record of what was described by local newspapers as the "most gruesome tragedy that Pittsburgh ever witnessed" by drawing together pieces of the story from contemporaneous local news accounts, existing public records and library materials. To the extent possible, original documents and records have been used to verify events, dates, names and places.

Over the last eight years, this story has evolved like a set of reverse nesting dolls. The smallest container, finding Grandpa's cousin, led to questions about the accident in general. The extent of death and serious injury to passengers and bystanders encouraged learning more about the victims. The immediate and angry community response after the accident prompted inquiry into local and state accident investigations and subsequent criminal and civil proceedings. The absence of formal public action against the Pittsburgh Railways Co. led to a look at the company's formation, its impact on public transportation and ultimately those who lived and worked in southwestern Pennsylvania.

Documented narratives create an accessible memory of a collective historical event. They allow us to weave the parts of a story together not only to tell what happened but also to build context and understanding about time and place. Our Kuffner family story grew from a search to find one person to a broader inquiry as the enormity of the individual victim stories emerged and news concerning the accident's aftermath unfolded. My interest in writing this story for a wider audience grew after the *Pittsburgh Post-Gazette* published my "The Next Page" article to commemorate the 100th anniversary of the Mount Washington Tunnel accident in December 2017 and readers contacted me to share their family connections to this story. I believe there are many more people with similar associations, and this book might link them to their part of a significant collective historical experience.

The introduction begins the story by providing context about life in Pittsburgh in 1917 and forms the setting for the accident.

Mary Jane Kuffner Hirt
April 2021

ACKNOWLEDGEMENTS

O ver the past nine years, my efforts to gather essential and relevant materials from archives and libraries in western Pennsylvania, Harrisburg, Philadelphia and St. Louis to effectively tell the story of the Mount Washington Tunnel accident have been well rewarded. Each interaction with a librarian or archivist became an opportunity to explore available resources, collect useful information and share the story. At no time did my requests for records or documents go unanswered or unfulfilled. The level of cooperation has been truly exceptional and genuinely appreciated. Their collective contributions reflect how this story evolved.

On December 26, 2011, I read newspaper microfilms at Carnegie Library in Oakland. By the end of the afternoon, I had solved the family mystery. During many return trips to the library, Amy Welch, Marilyn Holt and Gil Pietrzak, librarians in the Pennsylvania Department, have helped me fill in many details by helping to find books, photos or other materials. The Pennsylvania Department has been and will always be one of my favorite places to research!

The University of Pittsburgh's Archives and Special Collections offered a treasure-trove of what have become critical resources. Records from the Allegheny County Coroner's Office, the Pittsburgh Railways Co., early twentieth-century Hopkins maps and photos were made readily available by David Grinnell, the coordinator of Archives and Manuscripts, and library associate Laura Brooks. Their ongoing interest and enthusiasm made my visits to the archives service center pleasant and productive.

In the weeks following the accident, many victims and/or their families filed civil suits against the Pittsburgh Railways Co. Michael R. Murphy of the Allegheny County Court–Civil and Family Court Records division guided my initial search of the Adsectum Index to find case record numbers, and over the months it took to request and review civil case records, provided answers to many questions.

Surprising finds came from Ed Lybarger, the former archivist at the Pennsylvania Trolley Museum. Construction specifications, drawings and photos for the St. Louis Car Company's "Pittsburg" car from the museum's Pittsburgh Railways Co. collection nicely complemented the 4200 Series photos obtained from the Special Collections Department of the Library at Washington University in St. Louis.

The diverse array of resources from maps, reports and books to biographies of prominent Pittsburghers found at Heinz History Center's Detre Library and Archives help create and define the context of this story. The assistance, cooperation and enthusiasm of Chief Librarian Mary Jones and archivist Sierra Green over the last few years has been welcomed.

Special thanks to Robert Monks, Esq., at the Port Authority of Allegheny County, for providing scans of construction drawings of the early 1970s renovation of the Mount Washington Tunnel.

One of my last stops took me to the Allegheny County Court–Criminal Records office in search of documents about the prosecution of the trolley's motorman and conductor. Gary Nicotera's quick reply and gathering of the original court records filled a huge gap in this aspect of the story.

Understanding how the 1918 Pittsburgh Railways Co. bankruptcy affected the victims of the Mount Washington Tunnel accident was greatly facilitated by Gail Farr, archives specialist at the National Archives and Records Administration (NARA), in Philadelphia. Her initial overview of NARA's holdings on the case encouraged me to visit NARA to review ten boxes of material in which I ultimately found the list of claims made by the accident victims and their families.

This story went from an article to a book when Joe Smydo, the former editor of the *Pittsburgh Post-Gazette*'s "The Next Page," recognized there was more to this story than one newspaper article could tell.

I would truly be remiss if I did not acknowledge the contribution of numerous Pittsburgh newspaper reporters who followed this story in the days, weeks, months and years after December 24, 1917. The hundreds of articles most without bylines played a significant role in identifying the contours of this story.

And last but not least, sincere thanks to Patty, Judy, Kathy and Joan and many friends and family members who have provided encouragement during the time it has taken to write this story.

INTRODUCTION

PITTSBURGH, DECEMBER 1917

Pittsburgh as early as the mid-1700s was known for its location in the western foothills of the Allegheny Mountains and defined by the economic activity sustained by its three rivers; the Monongahela, Allegheny and Ohio; that converged adjacent to the city's central business district. Mount Washington, formerly called Coal Hill from its association with the nation's richest bituminous coal seam, rises steeply from the west bank of the Monongahela River. The city's hilly terrain affected industrial, commercial and residential development. Before 1920, expanding railroad, industrial and commercial activity pushed mill and factory workers and their families from the flat land near the rivers to the hillsides above the city where they lived in small, two-to two-and-a-half-story houses with party walls or freestanding homes built on narrow twenty-five-foot lots.

Federal census reports indicate that Pittsburgh and Allegheny County both experienced rapid population growth between 1900 and 1920. The county's population grew 53 percent from 775,000 to almost 1.2 million people, sufficient to make the county the fifth largest urban area in the country. The city's population increased 83 percent from 322,000 to 588,000 and made it the ninth largest city in the United States. The increase was driven the city's annexation of neighboring municipalities; Elliott, Esplen, Sheraden, Allegheny City, Brookline, Beechview and Spring Garden.

"Pittsburgh, Pennsylvania, View of Skyline," 1916. *Photo by J.J. Bauman, courtesy of Library of Congress Prints and Photographs Division.*

During the same time, immigration to the area generated by Pittsburgh-based mining and manufacturing companies labor recruitment efforts in Europe and the British Isles also contributed to the population surge. About 88 percent of the immigrants came from Germany, Poland, Italy, Ireland, Russia, Austria, Yugoslavia and Czechoslovakia and accounted for about 20 percent of the city and county's total population. Fifty-six percent of the immigrants soon became naturalized citizens.

By 1920, there were 255,788 families residing in Allegheny County with over 50 percent of the families living in the city of Pittsburgh. Although the average family had 4.68 members, the most common household size was 7 or more people and often included extended family members. The population was also relatively young with children under the age of eighteen comprising 34 percent of the city's population, while people forty-five or older constituted less than 20 percent. About 66 percent of county and 70 percent of city households rented rather than owned their homes. Since living within walking distance of one's place of employment was the norm, renting likely supported both job-related mobility and housing flexibility as family size changed.

ECONOMY

Economic activity was concentrated in the downtown area of the city. Pittsburgh had tall, steel-framed office buildings, magnificent department stores and grand railway terminals. Warehouses and factories occupied much of the land near the place where the rivers converged, while merchants sold and distributed their goods from warehouses and shops located along the Monongahela River side of the business district.

The region known in the nineteenth and early twentieth centuries as a center for the manufacture of pressed, cut, optical and window glass by 1917 had also experienced phenomenal growth in iron, steel and metal industries. Pittsburgh, described as a "city of steady, hardy men," had become the "workshop of the world." Mills connected by rail, river, telephone, telegraph and the U.S. Postal Service stretched outward from the city along the rivers for twenty miles. Bituminous coal mined throughout southwestern Pennsylvania powered trains; fueled iron, steel, coke and glass factories; generated electricity; and heated homes. As industrial production increased, the quality of the air deteriorated. Almost half of the days in 1915 were described as "smokey."

The local economy thrived in the early 1900s as 50 percent of all wage earners worked in heavy industry. Other important sectors included production related to meatpacking, baking, food processing, glass, optical goods and scientific instruments, petroleum refining, chemicals, paints, printing, automobile and rail car manufacturing and maintenance, electrical machinery and the manufacture of brass, bronze, tin and copper products.

In 1914, the Russell Sage Foundation studied the impact of Pittsburgh's pre–World War I industrial growth on the city's residents. The study drew two conclusions; life in the city was dominated by industrialists, the business community and political allies with interlocking corporate and financial interests and that there was a sharp contrast between the hardworking labor that supported economic prosperity and their living conditions that lacked basics such as fresh drinking water, sewage facilities, garbage collection and children's play areas.

DEMAND FOR PUBLIC TRANSPORTATION

The growth in the region's population and residential migration to neighborhoods beyond the city center created an increasing demand for consistent and affordable public transportation. The consolidated street railways system created by the Pittsburgh Railways Co., a subsidiary of the Philadelphia Company, by the early1900s became the primary mode of transit, especially for people who lived three or more miles from downtown.

By 1916, at its ridership peak, Pittsburgh Railways Co. streetcars transported 277 million passengers and traveled over four million car miles per year. Each day over 20 percent of the streetcar passengers traveled into and out of the city center to work or shop. Of the over eighty thousand workers who traveled to the city, 45 percent came from the east, 25 percent from the north, 16 percent from the south and 14 percent from the west. Pittsburgh's transit commissioner estimated that residents across Allegheny County rode trolleys 217 times per year. Streetcars had become an integral part of daily life.

As early as 1910, Allegheny County's consulting engineer, Edward Bigelow, concluded that the growing density of population, increasing need for efficient and effective transit and growing conflict among wagons, automobiles, trolleys and pedestrians created a huge problem on local streets that were generally too narrow and rarely had grades less than 5 percent.

Pittsburgh Street Traffic Congestion, 1916. *Reprinted from Electric Railway Transportation.*

Given its success in attracting riders from outlying areas and with encouragement from residential development companies, the Pittsburgh Railways Co. concentrated on building new routes into less populated areas rather than improving service on existing lines. By December 1917, the Pittsburgh Railways Co. generally attributed service-related issues to a lack of experienced personnel and limited operating revenues. The company's consistent failure to meet the demands and expectations of the public and municipal officials became a continuing source of tension and growing animosity among the parties.

In October 1916, Pittsburgh City Council allocated $68,000 for E.K. Morse, the city's transit commissioner, to investigate the volume, characteristics and movement of passenger traffic on street railways and steam railroads between the city and neighboring municipalities and develop reasonable options to achieve "rapid, efficient and cheap transit throughout the city and its suburbs." Morris and his staff were also tasked with the responsibility of considering the efficacy of private versus public transit system ownership, the coordination of existing transit systems and the economic and financial aspects of the problem. However, the Pittsburgh Railways Co. refused to participate in the study. The results of the transit report ultimately prompted the city to file a complaint with Pennsylvania Public Service Commission, asserting that the Pittsburgh Railways Co. failed to provide adequate service and citing the company's control of all service within the city, unjust fares, an inadequate transfer policy and its failure to properly maintain cars, tracks and roadways as significant problems.

Asserting that it could not to function within current operating revenue, on December 22, 1917, the Pittsburgh Railways Co. petitioned the Pennsylvania Public Service Commission for a fare increase from five to six cents.

NEWSPAPERS

In December 1917, three years before the introduction of radio, Pittsburgh area residents relied on morning and evening newspapers for local, national and international news. Local newspapers including the *Pittsburg Dispatch*, the *Pittsburgh Post*, the *Pittsburgh Sun*, the *Gazette Times*, the *Pittsburgh Chronicle Telegraph*, the *Hilltop Record* the *Pittsburg Press*, the *Pittsburgh Gazette* and the *Pittsburgh Leader* shared responsibility for communicating and ultimately

Photo by Holmes I. Mettee, American, 1881–
1947 (horse-drawn cart in road and industrial
complex in background, Pittsburgh) circa 1925,
gelatin silver print, H. 9 7/8 in. x W. 8 in.,
Carnegie Museum of Art, Pittsburgh.

preserving the details of significant events. By the end of 1917, World War
I and the its impact on the world, the country and the Pittsburgh region
consistently dominated the news.

WORLD WAR I—AN EARLY AND PROFOUND EFFECT ON PITTSBURGH

The men and women of the Pittsburgh region were significant contributors
to the war effort well before the United States became directly involved
in April 1917. Frank Murdock, in a speech to the Western Pennsylvania
Historical Society in 1921, recounted that after the war broke out in 1914,
Pittsburgh became a primary supplier of munitions for British, French,
Russian and Italian forces. Prior actions to increase industrial capacity by
building plants and installing equipment, coupled with the war production
experience of companies such as Westinghouse, ALCOA, Carnegie
Steel, PPG, Mesta Machine, Edgewater Steel, Heppenstall Forge & Knife
Co., National Tube, Universal Rolling Mill, Carbon Steel proved to be
extremely beneficial. The region became the "arsenal of the world" as
factories employing more than 500,000, worked day and night, seven
days per week, producing hundreds of millions of dollars of munitions,
armor plating, brakes for train locomotives and freight cars, gas masks,
optical glass for guns and rifles, tin cans for food, fans, wireless telegraph
and telephone instruments, electrical generators and unfinished steel for

manufacture by others. Pittsburgh's contribution to the war effort was believed to have been five to ten times greater than any other comparably sized city in the world.

In the years 1914 to 1919, 1,875 manufacturing companies located in the city saw a 20 percent increase in employment, from 69,620 to 83,290 with 143 companies employing 72 percent of the workers.

The value of manufacturing production in Pittsburgh during the war years increased almost 250 percent from $246.7 million to $614.7 million. About 68 percent of the total value was associated with iron and steel mills and machine shops. The remaining $195 million represented all other production.

Outside of Pittsburgh, eight hundred companies employed 90,271 people, with significant production located in Braddock, Duquesne, McKeesport, McKees Rocks, Homestead, Turtle Creek, North Braddock, Stowe and Swissvale.

A survey of 105 occupations in the thirty-five largest cities in the United States reported that hourly wages increased an average of 6 percent from 1916 to 1917, but noted that the average increase for metal industry workers was 13 percent. Part of the report looked at the hourly wage rates and hours worked per week for eighteen building and industry trades jobs in Pittsburgh. Hourly wages ranged from $0.44 to $0.70, and the work week averaged forty-four to seventy-five hours. Given the wage rates, Pittsburghers earned from $19.36 to $52.50 per week and were among the 74 percent of Pennsylvania wage earners who earned between $1,000 to $3,000 per year.

Four months after the United States entered World War I in April 1917, Allegheny County draft boards posted their initial lists of draftees. Most of the young men went on to serve in France as part of the U.S. Army's Twenty-Eighth and Eightieth Infantry Divisions. A second draft conducted in 1917 occurred in mid-December, with the expectation that 7,000 additional single men, without dependents, would be immediately called to service and transported to Fort Lee, Virginia for training. By Armistice Day in November 1918, 60,000 men from Allegheny County had served in the military, and 1,527 local lives were lost.

The increased demand for war related production combined with the draft of young men into military service caused labor shortages across the Pittsburgh area. Consequently, the Pennsylvania Bureau of Employment actively recruited women to fill jobs left vacant by men. By the end of 1917, 75,000 Allegheny County women had entered the workforce as hourly wage earners or volunteers in support of the war effort.

Left: In mid-1917, young men from the Pittsburgh region were drafted into the U.S. Army. *Photo from the George G. Bain Collection, "Pittsburgh soldier's good-by," circa 1915–circa 1920. Courtesy of Library of Congress Prints and Photographs Division.*

Below: The Pittsburgh Railways Co. advertised for woman to work as conductors. *Reprint from* Pittsburg Press, *December 4, 1917.*

WANTED.

Women to act as conductors on trippers and trailers in order to improve the service in the rush hours. Apply by letter in own handwriting to

EMPLOYMENT DEPARTMENT,
PITTSBURGH RAILWAYS COMPANY,
435 Sixth Ave.,   Pittsburg, Pa.

There is no doubt that the Pittsburgh Railways Co. suffered a severe loss of experienced workers to better-paying industrial jobs and the military draft. In December 1917, newspaper advertisements for men to work as motormen and women to work as conductors and maintenance personnel were prevalent.

Left: Children in the United States were encouraged to buy savings stamps to support the war effort. *Courtesy of Pennsylvania Historical and Museum Commission.*

Below: Red Cross Membership Drive, 1917. *Courtesy of Pennsylvania Historical and Museum Commission.*

Locally, the war affected the cost of living for local residents. Although food was not rationed, a 55 percent increase in the price of eggs, corn, wheat, sugar, oats, pork and beef and a 20 percent increase in the cost of milk, both well beyond the reported 6 percent average wage increase, effectively reduced consumption.

Coal for residential use was diverted to fuel heavy industry and generate electricity. But at the same time that local residents dealt with fuel shortages and rising food prices, they demonstrated their patriotism by purchasing war savings stamps to help fund the $32 billion war debt in amounts sufficient to rank third in the nation for per capita sales of the stamps.

Local Red Cross memberships also surged at the end of 1917 with 250,000 of the county's 255,788 households joining to confirm that the people back home were thinking about the boys in France who were spending Christmas away from home.

KNOXVILLE BOROUGH

The Knoxville #4236 streetcar line originated in Knoxville, a borough located atop Mount Washington, south of Pittsburgh's Allentown neighborhood, east of the Beltzhoover and Bon Air and west of Mount Oliver Borough. In the early 1900s, Knoxville was described as an ideal location for "thrifty, middle-class families." People were initially drawn to the community to work in its coal mines, brickyard, glassworks, shoe company, stone quarry and lumber mill.

From 1900 to 1920, the community's population doubled, growing from 3,511 to 7,201. At the time of the Knoxville trolley accident, about 40 percent of the borough's residents were immigrants or first-generation Americans. People generally traveled from Knoxville to the city by foot, horse-drawn wagon or trolley via routes that wound down the Mount Washington hillside. The town's newspaper, the *Hilltop Record*, in December 1904 reported that the opening of the Mount Washington Tunnel was enthusiastically welcomed as a tremendous time-saver.

During World War I, local historians noted that Knoxville's War Service Union mobilized the whole community in support of the war effort through its labor, financial assistance and civic involvement. Calls to ensure the "care and comfort of the local boys in the Army and Navy" and "perform any other service which might be useful to the nation" rallied the community.

CONCLUSION

Pittsburgh on Christmas Eve 1917 was a densely populated, busy, hardworking, diverse industrial community. The day was overcast and forty-eight degrees. Dueling banner headlines in the morning papers announced the civic, trade and business groups' intent to fight the recently announced

Pittsburgh Railways Co. fare increase and warned of the German Kaiser's threat of bold actions, if his demands for peace were not met.

The *Pittsburg Press* that day also reported that big pays had been distributed to workers over the prior two weeks and local residents had drawn out more than $1 million in Christmas savings. Hundreds of local soldiers returned to the area by train from Fort Lee, Virginia for five-day holiday furloughs before leaving for France. Much last-minute, hurried shopping and rushing to the post office to mail cards and packages marked the day. The city was looking forward to Christmas, when people would gather for church services, turkey dinners and enjoy time with family and friends.

In spite of all the attention to holiday preparations, the *Pittsburg Press* also affirmed that Christmas 1917 was a time of greater solemnity than Pittsburgh had known for a long while and expressed a hope that universal peace would be reached by the next year. In support of the military, community church bells were to toll in five-minute intervals from 7:30 to 8:00 p.m.

No one could have imagined the tragedy that would befall the city by late afternoon on Christmas Eve 1917.

PART I.

THE ACCIDENT

1
3:18 P.M., DECEMBER 24, 1917

Christmas Eve 1917 was a cold, rainy day in Pittsburgh. A crush of many last-minute shoppers, friends and family venturing out on holiday visits, along with men and women traveling to work, clambered onto the Pittsburgh Railways streetcar #4236 from stops along the Knoxville line just before 3:00 p.m. In addition to the crew, there were 114 fare-paying passengers, plus an unknown number who had transferred to the car before it reached the South Hills Junction. Motorman H.H. Klingler and conductor Martin Joyce took over the packed trolley at 3:04 p.m., a few minutes later than scheduled. About two hundred feet into the Mount Washington Tunnel, the trolley pole came off the wire. The car stopped, and the electric lights went out. The conductor, surrounded by the crowd in the middle of the car, could not leave the car to replace the trolley. The car sat in the dark for two to three minutes, until the motorman from a Charleroi car, LeRoy Hazelbacker, pulled up behind Knoxville #4236 and put the trolley pole back on the wire. When the lights came on, Motorman Klingler opened the controller to full speed, and the car leaped forward. The trolley was moving at a tremendous speed, rocking from side to side. The lights inside the tunnel streaked by as the car thundered down the steep grade. At the tunnel's North Portal, the car burst out of the darkness into the late afternoon light. When it reached the curve, the car left the tracks, darted down the slight grade to Carson Street and struck a fire hydrant, two utility poles and a peanut roaster at the Smithfield Confectionery. The trolley then slid one hundred feet across the

Knoxville #4236 Accident Scene, Smithfield and Carson Streets. *Reprint from* Gazette Times, *December 25, 1917.*

cobblestones and crashed into an iron fence in front of the Pennsylvania & Lake Erie Railroad (P&LE) terminal annex before the car turned over on its left side. As the trolley overturned, the screams of terrified passengers filled the air. The car hit the pavement with such force that it sounded like a bomb had exploded. Immediately after the impact, a dense cloud of dust rose from the wreckage. The trolley had crashed with the force of twelve to seventeen sticks of dynamite. The wreck left every window broken, much of the car's roof sheared off and its steel frame completely destroyed. Live electrical wires, unleashed by the runaway car and strewn across the intersection, posed additional danger to the passengers who survived the accident and those who came to their rescue.

Scenes inside the car were indescribable. The brutal crash caused unspeakable physical damage. Nearly every passenger was injured. Survivors of the tragedy told of the horror they felt when they saw the wrecked car and realized what had happened. Victims were literally torn to pieces or crushed and stripped of their clothing. Almost all sustained

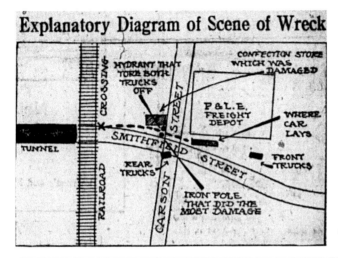

Left: The diagram provided details about the scene of the accident. *Reprint from* Pittsburg Dispatch, *December 25, 1917.*

Below: Interior of overturned Knoxville #4236 Car, Smithfield and Carson Streets. *Reprint from* Gazette Times, *December 25, 1917.*

cuts from shattered glass and splintered wood. Many with physical injuries also suffered from shock which made it more difficult for doctors to treat them at the scene.

Some, horribly crushed and trapped under the steel frame of the demolished car, cried out in pain or groaned softly as they waited for someone to rescue them. And some lay motionless in the wreckage. Hundreds of Christmas gifts covered with blood and mud lay on the cobblestones.

It was 3:18 p.m. Less than three minutes after the car entered the tunnel, fourteen people had died and over eighty were injured when Knoxville #4236, traveling at about five times the standard speed of ten miles per hour, crashed and became one of the worst transit accidents in the history of the city of Pittsburgh.

Within moments of the crash, P&LE Railroad employees and bystanders began working frantically to free the injured from the rubble. Within minutes, they were joined by police, firefighters, doctors and nurses who hurried to the scene.

Pittsburgh police officers **Charles A. Miller** and **James A. "Barney" Kilty**, stationed at the corner of Smithfield and Carson Streets, saw the accident and called the South Side station for help. Police and firefighters from all precincts and ambulances carrying nurses from South Side, St. Joseph's, Allegheny General and Mercy Hospitals hurried to the scene.

RESCUE EFFORT

Police commissioner Peter P. Walsh was returning by trolley from the city to his South Side district when the car stopped in the middle of the Smithfield Street Bridge. He jumped off the trolley and ran to see what had happened. He, too, called for all the police on the South Side as well as other stations. A few minutes later, Walsh, Lieutenant John Callan, Lieutenant Charles McAfee, Commissioner Robert J. Alderdice and Commissioner Charles Johnston found themselves struggling to hold back the massive crowd that descended on the scene and made the rescue work extremely difficult.

Minutes later, Mayor Joseph G. Armstrong, Coroner Samuel C. Jamison, public safety director Charles S. Hubbard and police superintendent W. Noble Matthews arrived on the scene to take over crowd control and oversee rescue efforts.

"My God!" yelled a firefighter to Commissioner Walsh and Mayor Armstrong as he picked up a head and a leg from the inside of the car. "It's awful, awful," said the mayor, who added, "This will be a sad Christmas for the families of these people" as he directed the firefighters to place the body parts in the morgue ambulance.

Shortly after city council convened, it learned of the tragedy. Council president James P. Kerr, a physician at St. Joseph's Hospital, requested the meeting be adjourned. Then he rushed to the scene.

Rescuers lifted the victims through three windows in the front of the overturned car and placed them on the sidewalk at the entrance of the P&LE annex or carried them inside, where railroad employees administered first aid. Victims were also taken to the Pennsylvania Railroad warehouse, the P&LE freight station, the Smithfield Confectionery and other stores and hotels in the neighborhood.

RESCUERS TELL OF EXPERIENCES

A most compelling account of the accident came from **Andrew L. Deckenbaugh**, chief clerk at the P&LE freight office, the building where the front of the car ultimately came to rest. "I dashed to the window the second I heard the crash which sounded like a bomb," said Deckenbaugh. "For a moment all I could see was a cloud of dust." When the dust settled, "I saw that the streetcar was completely demolished." He recalled that the passengers lay in a huddled mass, unable to move inside the car. Children screamed for their mothers. Women cried out for help. A man climbed out from the mound of bodies, "kicking others in the face as he worked himself free." Many bystanders and men from nearby shops rushed to the scene. But when they got closer, they found the wreckage so horrible that all they could do was wring their hands and frantically run from one end of the car to the other.

Deckenbaugh then recounted that every freight office employee "was there in less time than it takes to tell." The terminal annex served as a temporary hospital. As quickly as the injured were removed from the debris, they were taken upstairs and placed on tables, where a dozen first aid teams under the direction of Dr. John D. Milligan, the P&LE's in-house doctor, worked with doctors from South Side, Mount Washington and Duquesne Heights and doctors and nurses from local hospitals to treat the injured before they were taken to hospitals or sent home. Deckenbaugh stated, "Once the injured had been removed, we could see how many were dead. We moved the dead to the curb. They were later taken to the morgue."

By the end of the day, hundreds of people had rushed to the PL&E building searching for missing relatives. To help locate family members, the staff compiled a list of victims and the hospitals where they were taken and helped those who escaped serious injury telephone home.

Deckenbaugh concluded his comments by saying, "I shall never forget the scenes I witnessed during the work of rescue. A mob of persons from nowhere suddenly descended upon us demanding to see and know all about the accident. By this time, a score of policemen had come and they beat back the crowd and attempted to restore order. Traffic was not closed, however, and it is a wonder many more were not hurt from the resultant confusion."

Long-term P&LE freight employee **Bernard C. McMeal** was one of the first to reach the wrecked car. He carried many victims into the building. After a time, the exhausting work and horrific sights took their toll. On returning to the scene after carrying a dead woman into the building, he fainted and struck his head on the cobblestone pavement. After being treated for a head wound, McMeal was taken to his home.

The crash did not initially alarm P&LE clerk **Christopher G. Vogel**. He thought rail cars moving in the freight yard had hit hard when coupling. When Vogel reached the street, "he found the framework of the car a mere splintered shell." He described the victims as "a seething mass of groaning, screaming, struggling human beings," and at times, he had to avert his eyes and "grit his teeth" to continue. After all the victims were removed, he went back to look at the wreckage. Bloodstained hats of all shapes and sizes and hundreds of brightly wrapped packages ready for delivery or mailing to friends and loved ones were scattered about the pavement. He said, "[T]he front trucks of the car had broken loose. The front end of the car, where it struck the telegraph pole, was smashed in. The whole top was sheared off. The steel pole…was bent low." The awning on the corner store was broken down and covered with mud.

Many other P&LE accounting department employees also witnessed the accident. They quickly joined in the rescue effort. When their work was finished, many were covered with soil and blood and looked like they, too, had been lifted from the demolished car.

P&LE clerks David. P. Weis and Roy W. May were hesitant to comment. Weis described the experience of "seeing many bodies with heads either torn off or smashed to a pulp…and the appearance of limbs almost cut from bodies, or so badly crushed as to bear no resemblance to arms or legs" as horrific.

Others from the PL&E office who helped rescue or care for the injured included William Neunze, Lewis Eader, Walter Fry, John Nessle, Frank Rodgers and Issac Pearlman.

When **M.E. Shipp**, a Pittsburgh Railways Co. inspector located at the north end of the tunnel, realized the trolley was out of control, he was able to disperse the crowd waiting at the Birmingham Station, except for one woman. Shipp said she appeared "bewildered and remained stationary" in spite of his frantic effort to make her get out of the way. She did not heed his warning. When the car left the track and rolled over, she was crushed against a telegraph pole. The woman was later identified as Clara Tanney.

Charles Walsh, age thirty-five, a Pennsylvania Railroad purchasing agent, was standing on the corner of Smithfield and Carson Streets when the car plunged out of the tunnel. "So fast was it going that I jumped back from the curb, startled by the speed of its rush toward me. A moment later it literally leaped from the tracks as it struck the curve…skidded sideways" and turned over with such force that it "shook the street. The momentum was so great that even after it was on its side it continued to skid toward the sidewalk until it struck the front railing in front of the railroad building." Walsh continued, "I lifted from the mass of wreckage one Negro woman whose head had been crushed almost unrecognizably. There is no hope that she can live. Altogether, I took four dead persons from the end of the car in which I was working. It was the most terrible scene I have ever witnessed."

William Smith Jr. stood a few feet from where the car collided with the iron pole. He told Coroner Jamison that he alone pulled out twelve women from the wreckage, and three of them were dead.

Eugene Vey, a private at Camp Lee, was home on a furlough and was passing the tunnel in his automobile when the accident occurred. He helped remove the dead and injured from the wreck and later carried several loads of injured people to the hospital.

Interviews with passengers who survived the crash uninjured presented consistent descriptions of the circumstances that led up to replacing the trolley after the car stopped. They said people were packed into the car when it left the car barn at the south of the Mount Washington Tunnel. All recalled the trolley came off the wire and lights went out soon after Knoxville #4236 entered the tunnel. The conductor was wedged in by the crowd and could not leave the car to replace the trolley. The motorman and conductor had a somewhat heated exchange. The conductor told the motorman to replace the trolley, but before the motorman could do so a Charleroi car came up behind the Knoxville car and its motorman put the trolley on the wire. When the electric came on, the motorman threw on the power at full speed, and the car lunged forward. The passengers believed the motorman, in an attempt to make up lost time, accelerated too quickly. The "car gathered momentum with such rapidity that the passengers felt something was wrong." Many concerned comments were overheard. When the passengers realized the car was beyond control, because the aisles were densely packed, there was no scrambling to leave the car, even though many believed an accident was imminent. The trolley dashed through the tunnel at a "horrific" speed and shot out of the north end like a "huge projectile." It did not seem any of the brakes were applied until the car reached the lower end of the tunnel, when the car slowed up somewhat. There was little screaming. There was no panic. The crash came so suddenly that none could recall anything immediately preceding it. Instead, the passengers described a common physical experience: "the sensation of the rush through the tunnel, the sickening dip down the tunnel mouth grade, and then the shock and terror and pain as the car leaped from the runways, the momentary sickness of the jolting plunge, and then the crash."

Pittsburgh-Post stereotyper **John P. O'Malley** was on his way to work. O'Malley said, "The car swayed to one side just as it rushed out of the tunnel and the next thing I remember was sliding along over the pavement on top of three or four other passengers."

H.B. Carroll, who later became a critical eyewitness in the state's investigation, escaped with minor injuries. Carroll, a P&LE Railroad engineer, harshly criticized the crew's refusal to adjust the trolley pole. He explained, "When we were about halfway through the tunnel the trolley came off. The conductor, hemmed in on all sides by the crowd, was unable to leave the car. After making several unsuccessful attempts to elbow his way through the jam, he cried to the motorman, 'Will you get off and put the trolley on? I can't get out.' 'Put it on yourself; that is your duty,' the motorman answered." After the motorman refused to reattach the trolley, Carroll said, "The car remained stationary for about two minutes, until the Charleroi car came up behind us." The motorman of that car realized what was wrong and put the trolley back on the wire. The motorman then "threw on his power and away we went at a terrible speed." According to Carroll, the first indication "that the car was beyond the motorman's control was when I saw him working frantically at his brakes....When the car left the tracks, I saw the motorman stationed at his post and he was there when the crash came." Carroll was thrown to the rear of the car and escaped by crawling through a broken window. He then helped rescue other passengers.

Nelson Vance Shook said that he was seated behind the conductor when the accident occurred. "It is my opinion that the motorman wanted to make up the time lost, as he started the car a terrific speed," said Shook. "We traveled down the tunnel grade at least fifty miles an hour. As the car reached the north end of the tunnel the motorman made an effort to apply the brakes, but it was too late. Then the crash came. I was unconscious for a few minutes. After recovering I reached the shattered windows and pulled myself through mangled bodies. Women screamed and men rushed wildly over scores of injured passengers. I never want to see such a sight again."

The *Pittsburgh Dispatch* reported that "an un-named child, age 9, escaped death or serious injury when the car struck the steel pole. The boy had five cents and was about to put it into the cup next to the peanut roaster in front of the confectionary store. A clerk in the store, J. Maloney, said as the boy reached into the roaster for a package of peanuts, he saw the trolley, screamed, dropped the peanuts and ran to the other side of the curb just before the car crashed into the peanut roaster."

SOLDIER ACTED

The tragedy was not shielded from criminal opportunists. The *Pittsburgh Post* reported that an individual tried to take advantage of victims by posing as a rescue worker. Instead of helping, he stole jewelry and purses from injured women. An unnamed soldier saw what was happening and "grabbed the man by the back of the neck and dragged him behind a nearby signboard where he gave him a sound thrashing."

TRANSPORTING THE VICTIMS

Most of the dead and injured were women and children. To speed up the removal of the seriously injured to hospitals and return those with minor injuries to their homes, police commandeered private automobiles, delivery trucks and wagons coming and going to the city from the South Side. Private vehicles transported almost sixty victims to city hospitals, Mercy Hospital, twelve; St. Joseph's Hospital, twenty; South Side Hospital, twenty-five; and Allegheny General Hospital, two.

Two large delivery trucks filled with Christmas packages had to be unloaded first. The dead and the seriously injured were then stacked on top of each other and the drivers were directed to hurry to St. Joseph's Hospital. Dr. Harry Felton, in addition to treating victims at the scene, loaded many into his "machine" and made several trips to the South Side and St. Joseph's Hospitals. Two Pittsburgh Railways Co. emergency wagons were also pressed into service.

Then came the heartrending responsibility of notifying the families of the dead and injured.

The news of the Knoxville #4236 accident spread through the city like wildfire. Not long after the accident, hundreds of anxious people arrived at the morgue and hospitals in automobiles, streetcars and on foot. The *Gazette Times* reported that "at the hospitals, it took scores of police to keep the crowds from entering the institutions and interfering with the work of physicians." At South Side and St. Joseph's Hospitals, where most of the injured were taken, people were lined up for two blocks waiting to find out if any of their relatives or friends were among the injured. Due to difficulty in obtaining the names and addresses of patients, only partial lists were prepared by hospital staff and were passed out by the police to the public as eight or ten people were identified. Most often, the concerns of family or friends were unwarranted. But all too often, the cry of a woman or man signaled a loved one had been found. These people were then permitted to enter the hospital, while the others rushed on to the other hospitals. Even if a loved one was not found, many still feared the worst and remained inconsolable. One such family member, Joseph Tanney, searched for several hours to find his wife who was supposed to have met him at 3:30 p.m. at the corner where the car overturned. He found her in the morgue. She had been identified a short time before by her brother, John C. McGrath. Doctors on Christmas Eve night reportedly treated many cases of extreme anxiety.

Police vehicles and the morgue ambulance were tasked with moving those who had died to the morgue on Diamond Street. "The first eight bodies taken to the morgue were those of women who had perished in the accident." All had died from fractured skulls resulting when their heads hit the car's steel structure when the car turned onto its side. When the ambulance arrived at the morgue and the bodies of the first two women were removed and taken into the mortuary, the crowd of men was overcome with emotion and began to sob. Moments later, when the police brought in two more women, much of the crowd grasped the horrific nature of the accident and moved farther away from the building. When two more police vehicles, each with two more bodies, backed into the morgue's receiving area, the last of the onlookers disappeared.

Generally stoic morgue deputies were seen turning away to wipe away tears as relatives or friends provided proof of identification for those who had died in the accident. Most of the dead were identified by the words, "Yes, those are the clothes she wore."

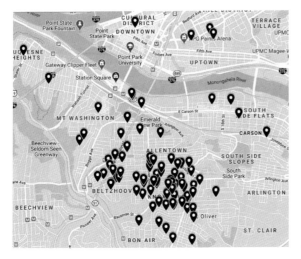

Residential locations, Knoxville #4236 accident victims. Mapping the victims' home addresses demonstrates the accident's impact. Over 95 percent of the victims resided within the city of Pittsburgh or boroughs adjacent to the city. Over 50 percent lived in neighborhoods closest to the Knoxville trolley route—Beltzhoover (four deaths, eighteen injured); Knoxville (nine deaths, thirty-five injured); and Mount Oliver (two deaths, ten injured). *Illustration by author.*

Twenty-three women, children and men ultimately died as a consequence of the Knoxville #4236 trolley accident. Fifteen died on Christmas Eve: William Bolitho, Eugene Bricmont, Mabel Brecht, Aurelia Czerny, Pauline Dewmyer, Caroline M. Fischer, Sidney H. Frank, Howard E. Ford, Wesley Jones, Sarah Kirkham, Mathilda Klinzing, Clara Miller, Ella Sheridan, Clara Tanney and Rose Zurlinden. Four died on Christmas Day: James Cosgrove, Josephine Retzbach, Clara Rushway and Elizabeth J. Patterson. Two died on December 26 and 27: Adele Bongiovanni and Robert Rosenfelter. And the twenty-second and twenty-third deaths came in January 1918, with the passing of two children, Elmer A. McCoy Jr. and Gladys E. Sheridan.

INTO THE NIGHT

Even as police, firefighters and civilians worked to rescue the dead and injured, the Pittsburgh Railways Co. wrecking crews and inspectors started to collect the remnants of the accident and clear away the wreckage. A Pittsburgh Railways freight car was filled with the blood-soaked clothing and belongings of the dead and injured. A satchel filled with women's pocketbooks and many neatly wrapped Christmas packages was taken to the South Side police station, where investigators at the request of coroner's office had already begun to search for various pieces of "jewelry, pocketbooks containing large sums of money, valuable furs and clothing which had disappeared immediately after the accident." Of the many items reported missing, Deputy Coroner Hugh Dempsey specifically noted that Caroline Fischer's pocketbook containing $100 in cash and a Liberty bond and Jennie Mercer's $600 Sunburst brooch with opals and pearls were missing. Since bystanders had already turned articles of clothing, bags and suitcases over to the morgue, he hoped people who might have picked up other items would follow suit.

A large gravel car used for construction work was loaded with pieces of debris, some of which was found forty yards from the accident scene. Working late into the night on Christmas Eve under difficult conditions, Pittsburgh Railways Co. maintenance employees removed the shell of the wrecked car from the intersection. The car's rear trucks (wheels) lay on Carson Street near the tunnel exit, while the front trucks, still attached to the car, lay at the front door of the Pittsburgh terminal annex. Remnants of the roof from the middle and rear of the car sat in a pile on the southern side of Carson Street. The iron pole was bent but still standing, while only a stump of the wooden pole remained.

By 6:00 p.m., less than three hours after the crash, the tunnel reopened to South Hills streetcars going in and out of the city. The next day, after all of the rubble had been removed, the only evidence of the accident was a damaged iron railing in front of the P&LE terminal annex building.

On Christmas Eve, the Pittsburgh Railways Co. issued a statement acknowledging the deaths and injuries and promised to undertake a thorough accident investigation.

Coroner Samuel C. Jamison, after visiting St. Joseph's Hospital at 8:00 p.m. on Christmas Eve, reported that twenty-five additional doctors were called in to help dress wounds and try every way possible to save the lives of the injured. He also issued a statement to the community: "Our first duty is to take care of the dead and injured, which we are doing to the best of our ability with the help of the medical fraternity, hospitals and undertakers, who have been more than zealous in their efforts to relieve the pain and suffering of the injured and to assuage the sorrow of the bereaved. We have several theories as to the cause of the disaster, which we are investigating in order to arrive at the proper conclusion and to place the blame where it belongs."

City residents, especially those of Knoxville, were stunned by the news of the car disaster. On Christmas Day, as caskets stood in darkened parlors in place of gaily decorated Christmas trees and families across Mount Washington planned funerals that would mark the rest of the holiday week,

The Pittsburgh Post

WEDNESDAY MORNING, DECEMBER 26, 1917.

TWO CENTS.

WRECK WHICH KILLED 19 IS PROBED BY CORONER AND PUBLIC SERVICE COMMISSION

FIXED PRICE FINAL DRIVE SAVES U.S. FOR DRY 30-CENT NATION

BLACK CLOUD OF TRAGEDY DARKENS CHRISTMAS DAY IN HOMES OF KNOXVILLE

U.S. SOLDIER VICTIM OF CRUELTY

ITALIANS RETAKE ASIAGO

The Allegheny County coroner and Pennsylvania Public Service Commission acted quickly to fix the blame for the Knoxville #4236 trolley accident. Pittsburgh Post, *December 26, 1917*.

the investigation to fix responsibility for the accident had commenced. **John P. Dohoney**, the Pennsylvania Public Service Commission's chief investigator was dispatched from Harrisburg to join Allegheny County officials and Pittsburgh Railways Co. representatives in an inspection of the crash site and examination of the wreckage.

Note—Crash Impact: When interviewed after the accident, several bystanders compared the impact of the streetcar crashing onto Carson and Smithfield Streets to a bomb exploding. The force of the crash can be measured by considering the weight of the car (88,000 pounds); the estimated weight of the passengers, their possessions and packages (17,800 pounds); and the speed at which the car was presumably traveling (estimated prior to impact as fifty to sixty miles per hour). The results of the calculation indicate that the energy of the collision at fifty miles per hour (analogous to force) would be equivalent to the explosion of 11.99 sticks of dynamite; at fifty-five miles per hour as 14.51 sticks of dynamite; and at sixty miles per hour as 17.26 sticks of dynamite. A further comparison suggests that the intensity of the crash was comparable to blowing up thirteen to nineteen tons of rock.

2

THE WHOLE CITY GRIEVED

The mourners in the stricken homes had what consolation there was in knowing that the entire city sorrowed with them and that no home was untouched by the gloom of the tragedy. Now the call is for rendering any practical help that may be necessary. See that none of the injured or the families of the dead suffers for anything that can be supplied by a sympathetic and generous community
— *"The Holiday Tragedy,"* Pittsburgh Post, *December 28, 1917*

Many men left their homes atop Mount Washington on Christmas Eve morning bound for jobs in the city with the expectation that other family members would take a streetcar into town during the afternoon. As the news of the accident swept across the city, for many, a great sense of relief replaced overwhelming dread when loved ones were found unharmed. For others, the sense of dread turned to grief for those who had perished or concern about those who were gravely injured. Reports of the accident immediately permeated the crowds at markets and in stores as they made last-minute holiday purchases. It was a sad day for all in Pittsburgh.

In Knoxville Borough, scarcely a home was left untouched by the tragedy. Those without family members among the victims mourned the loss or injury of close neighbors. So widespread was the sorrow of the community that its people regarded the accident as one shared by all as neighbor helped neighbor by taking care of children or household chores while families prepared for funerals or tended to the injured at home or in hospitals. Households where Christmas was truly celebrated were few and far between

"Bobbie" Mallory. *Reprint from* Pittsburg Dispatch, *December 25, 1917.*

that year. The holiday spirit, Christmas trees and gifts were generally abandoned for funeral flowers. Crêpe hung beside holly. Blinds on windows darkened parlors where the remains of loved ones rested on biers. In the homes where holiday preparations were complete, the cries of joy from small children on Christmas morning served to heighten the pain felt by the adults around them as they realized that no gift could make up for their loss. Christmas 1917 would be marked by indelible memories for years to come.

In the first forty-eight hours after the accident, local newspapers told two stories, one about the accident and its immediate aftermath and the other about the victims and their rescuers. In numerous brief sketches, some with photographs, readers learned that the dead and injured represented all sectors of society. In many instances, the details of the descriptions, woven together with care by their authors, created distinctive, compelling and lasting impressions of the victims, their families and friends. The stories bring the tragedy to life.

Bobbie Mallory and **Eddie Carter** were on their way downtown after delivering Christmas gifts in Knoxville. Bobbie received a five-dollar gift, and the boys were intent on spending the money. After the wreck, Bobbie, in serious condition with a broken wrist and lacerated head, was taken to South Side Hospital. At the South Side police station, Eddie sat crying and clutching his friend's hat. "I don't know how I escaped," he cried, "because I was sitting beside Bobbie when the car turned over. I crawled out over the top and ran away and cried." Later it was reported that Alec Alpern, age eight, and Ralph Trolilo, age eleven, camped out at South Side Hospital until hospital personnel relented and permitted the boys to visit their "chum" Bobbie. All of the boys lived in the Lower Hill District.

Knoxville resident **Marcella Dueck**, age fifteen, attributed the accident to the railway's practice of packing people into cars like "sardines." Initially, she was in the rear of the car but was pushed toward the front as more people boarded. Moving forward likely saved her from death or serious injury. Dueck said the passengers were concerned about how fast the car was going but generally were not excited. "The car rocked slightly as it neared the end of the tunnel, and then leaped from the track. Everything

Marcella Dueck. *Reprint from* Pittsburg Dispatch, *December 25, 1917.*

Howard Young. *Reprint from* Pittsburgh Post, *December 25, 1917.*

grew dark and I felt myself falling. I was buried among many people, and after desperate efforts, managed to pull myself out of the heap of mangled bodies. I saw terrible sights all around me, sights that I shall never be able to forget. It is impossible to describe the awful mutilation of the bodies of the women," many of whom she knew from the Knoxville and Mount Oliver. The *Pittsburgh Post* later reported that as Dueck climbed from the rubble, she handed her purse and a package to a man standing nearby. When she recovered from the shock of the ordeal, she realized the man and her possessions were gone.

The youngest victim, **Howard Young**, age nine, was sent to town from his Beltzhoover home for a haircut. Howard escaped being crushed to death because he was sitting on the conductor's seat behind the fare box in the middle of the car between a woman and the conductor. For a child, his description of the accident was quite explicit. He said he had never seen so many people on the car and explained that just after the car exited the north end of the tunnel and went under the PA Railroad bridge, some of the wheels seemed to go out from under the car. The car left the inbound track and appeared to move over to the outbound track. Then, the car leaned toward the P&LE station, struck something and turned on its side. Howard was buried in the car when it overturned. The conductor was wedged in behind him, and a woman laying on top of him was lifeless and cut "something awful." (He learned later that she had died.) When he saw a hole cut in the car, he crawled over the dead and injured people and started out. When he was about halfway out, a man, later identified as **James F. McCann**, caught hold of him and pulled him the rest of the way out. Howard had a bruise over his eye and a cut cheek. His coat was covered with blood, and he had lost his hat. He asked if someone could telephone his parents. As he hurried up the street, someone yelled, "Where you going?" Howard replied, "My mother told me to get my haircut—that's where I'm going," and away he went. He was the son of Howard S. and Gertrude W. Brandt Young.

Mount Washington resident **Charles Roberts**, age thirty-four, a freight conductor for the P&LE Railroad, was one of the first to climb out of the car. A bit unsteady, he rested for a few minutes beside the car and drank some brandy provided by someone rendering first aid. Limping but cheerful, he went into the Smithfield Confectionery and called his wife. He told his wife, Ella, "I'm all right, just called you up to tell you I was in a little wreck down here, but I'm just shook up, I guess I'll be home after a while." Then he wavered and dropped the telephone receiver. Roberts shouted to a clerk that he was tired and needed a chair. He dropped into the chair, and the police were called. He was taken to Southside Hospital and treated for a back injury. All the while, his wife was unaware. She said her husband had suddenly hung up but thought he might just have been nervous. When he didn't return home by 9:00 p.m., she started to search the hospitals. Neither the police nor a hospital had contacted her. Roberts lived on Ruxton Avenue and had four children, Stewart, age eight; Mary Jane, six; Gene, two; and Keith, one.

Beltzhoover resident **Mrs. Frances "Harry" Schulze** said the passengers were packed in "like cattle" and heard several people say the motorman was attempting to make up for lost time. When the car crashed, she was thrown to the bottom of the car and felt like she was slowly suffocating. She pushed her head up through the layers of bodies lying on top of her to get some air. Most of the people were still, their heads down and feet in the air. She saw some terrible sights. No one appeared to be all right. A man near her had "blood pouring from his face, making it unrecognizable." She asked him to help her. "He caught my arm and drew me towards the top of the heap of bodies and I scrambled to the top of the car," she said. "As I stood there for a moment, I heard some people yell at me to jump, but I don't know how I made my way to the street." After treatment at the terminal annex, Mrs. Schulze was taken home, where she later suffered a nervous breakdown.

Morris Julius and **George Birmingham** were traveling south toward the tunnel. Their express wagon had just crossed Carson Street when the trolley shot from the tunnel. Although Julius was facing the tunnel, he said he did not see the trolley until it crashed into the pole a few feet in front of him. His wagon was struck before it overturned. The horse was hit first. Then the horse, wagon and Julius were thrown to the right side of the street. Julius

Elmer McCoy Jr. *Courtesy of Bill McKeown.*

landed on his head and was knocked unconscious. Birmingham, a passenger on the wagon, was thrown to the left, toward the overturned trolley. Julius said Birmingham appeared to be dead until he gasped when he was lifted from the pavement. The horse died of severe head injuries.

Some stories really stay with you. That of Elmer A. McCoy Jr. is one such example. The **McCoy** boys, **Elmer A. Jr.**, age ten, and **Matthew**, age eight, visited their uncle Samuel J. McCoy's home at 510 Cedarhurst Street,

Beltzhoover, on Christmas Eve morning to deliver gifts. Passengers recalled the boys being gleeful when they got on the trolley. Mr. McCoy had given Elmer an air rifle, "his heart's desire, which he displayed with boyish pride." When Annie McCoy, the boys' mother, heard about the accident, she was certain the boys were on the trolley and immediately began searching local hospitals. When she arrived at St. Joseph's Hospital, she was described as "near collapse." She pleaded for help to find Elmer and Matthew. Hospital staff, after making numerous telephone calls, found the children at the P&LE station. Without waiting to hear more, Annie rushed to the terminal annex. She found that both boys had been injured. Matthew was treated for minor head injuries and released. Elmer had compound skull fractures and gashes in his face that required scores of stitches.

Over the days following the accident, local newspapers kept in touch with Elmer's parents, who were constantly at his bedside. The boy was said to have been unconscious except for a moment on Christmas Day when he opened his eyes and spoke the word "Daddy."

Elmer was described as a cheerful and bright boy, the head of his class in school. His father, Elmer A. McCoy Sr., said, "He could go anywhere, for he was so quick and bright. He went to Sharon every summer alone." Elmer Jr., after faithfully practicing with others in the choir, had looked forward to singing at the Christmas service at St. Mary's Church.

A last-minute decision by their parents to take little sister, Anna, age six, shopping for a new coat rather than going with the boys to Beltzhoover likely saved her from injury or death.

Elmer died on January 9, 1918, at South Side Hospital and was the accident's twenty-second fatality. The McCoy family resided at 4600 Penn Avenue, Bloomfield, across from St. Mary Catholic Cemetery, where Elmer is buried. Elmer A. McCoy Sr. was a conductor on the Pittsburgh Railways Hamilton Avenue line.

At the Jacob Fischer home in Knoxville, the family and relatives mourned the loss of daughter Caroline. Confined to her home with a severe cold for almost a week, she left her sickbed on Christmas Eve to purchase gifts for her nieces and

Miss Caroline Fischer.

Caroline Fischer. *Reprint from* Gazette Times, *December 26, 1917.*

nephews. After stopping at a bank in Knoxville, she traveled into the city with a neighbor, Laura Ohl. **Caroline Fischer** was a well-known and respected teacher at the Birmingham School in South Side. She became an ardent Red Cross volunteer after her brothers Howard and Charles were drafted into the army. In addition to knitting sweaters and wristlets for American soldiers, she managed a war savings stamp buying program for her fourth-grade pupils. Caroline was the oldest of Jacob and Julia Fischer's eight children: John W., William H., Howard W., Charles F., Clara Edgar, Bertha Meyers and Edna. She was a member of the Knoxville Presbyterian Church.

Wesley Jones.

Wesley Jones. *Reprint from* Gazette Times, *December 26, 1917.*

Wilkes-Barre native **Wesley Jones**, age twenty-one, worked as a stenographer for the Bessemer and Lake Erie Railroad and lived with his brother and sister-in-law Roland and Marian Jones in Knoxville. Wesley was a kind and funny person. Just before he left home on Christmas Eve to buy gifts for his little niece and nephew, he entertained his sister-in-law by dancing in the hallway. On his way down the street, he stopped to tease a little neighbor boy. They both laughed, and Wesley continued on, whistling as always. Monday night, Marian Jones and her children eagerly awaited the return of Wesley and Roland. When the doorbell rang, Marian, aware of the accident, immediately realized that the strangers at her door were connected to the tragedy. Wesley had died at St. Joseph's Hospital on Monday at 4:10 p.m. His body was identified from the bank book he carried.

Wesley Jones wanted to be a soldier and tried to enlist several times, but the tall and slender young man was judged too frail by army doctors. Just recently, though, he was drafted and looked forward to serving his country in some way. After graduating from the Wilkes-Barre Business College, the well-known and popular young man moved to Knoxville. His parents, William and Elizabeth Jones, brother James and sister Annie, lived in Westmore, Luzerne County.

William R. Bolitho went into the city on Christmas Eve to buy more trimmings for the family's tree. Fifteen-month-old William Jr. watched at the front window, awaiting his father's return, and kept asking his mother, Amelia, why his father wasn't trimming the tree. On Christmas, the half-decorated tree stood in the corner of the dining room of the Bolitho's Knoxville home. William Bolitho's casket lay in the parlor.

Born in Wales, Bolitho immigrated to the United States with his parents, Thomas and Jane Bolitho, at age three. Living in Allegheny County most of his life, he was a graduate of Carnegie Institute of Technology and was employed as a sheet metal worker. He had recently passed the draftsman's examination. Earlier on Christmas Eve, the postman had delivered an army service questionnaire for Mr. Bolitho. His wife was so stricken that she collapsed.

Mr. Bolitho was survived by his parents; three sisters, Mary B. (Ellis) Rush, Hettie (Morley) Eisele of Pittsburgh and Eva (Samuel) Rush of Uniontown; and a brother, Thomas B. Bolitho of Carrick.

When Jane Kirkham learned of the trolley accident, she had a premonition that her daughter had been injured. Little did she know that **Sarah Kirkham**, age twelve, had died in the accident. Her father, Walter B. Kirkham, a *Pittsburgh Dispatch* cashier, positively identified her body at the morgue from her clothing. He later related that, uncharacteristically, his wife had telephoned him from their Bon Air home to ask whether their daughter had yet arrived at his Fifth Avenue office. Jane reported that there had been an accident and feared that their daughter was injured. Mature for her age, Sarah was often sent on errands to the city. On Christmas Eve, Sarah was continuing to help prepare for the family's Christmas when she arranged to meet her father about 4:00 p.m. at his office to go shop for a few last-minute gifts. When Jane found that Sarah was not with her father, she insisted that he begin a search. When his calls to local hospitals proved unsuccessful, he contacted the police and Pittsburgh Railways to see whether Sarah was among those killed. Since devastating injuries made identification difficult, no list of deaths was available. For a time, Walter thought his daughter might have escaped unharmed but deep-down knew that if that were true, Sarah certainly would have arrived at his office. At 5:00 p.m., he walked to the morgue on Diamond Street, where he found his daughter. His search was over; his wife's worst fears had come true. Telling Jane that Sarah was gone was a most difficult task; his wife collapsed from the shock when she heard the horrifying details and was reported to be in serious condition.

Sarah, one of the Beltzhoover School's brightest pupils, was thought to have a promising future. A member of the Knoxville Chorus, she was sorely missed at their holiday concert. One of four children, she had two brothers, LeRoy M. and Walter, and a sister, Anna.

One of the saddest of stories is that of **Pauline Dewmyer**, age fifty-three, and **Sidney H. Frank**, age forty-eight. She was employed as a carpet sewer by the Joseph Edmundson Co., and he worked as a machinist in the Altoona shop of the PA Railroad. They were engaged and on their way to Pittsburgh to shop for her Christmas gift after visiting Norman B. Anderson. The ride through the tunnel would be the happy couples' last few minutes together.

Dewmyer's body was the first removed from the wreckage. She lived with her sisters, Kate Dewmyer and Maggie Jackson, at 600 Fifth Avenue, McKeesport. Frank lived long enough to be taken to St. Joseph's Hospital. When Frank left his home at 1922 Fifth Avenue, Altoona, he sent his two sons, Earl, age eighteen, and William, age ten, and daughter, Lillian, sixteen, to visit his mother, Catherine Frank, in Johnstown. He planned to meet the children at the Johnstown railroad station on Christmas Eve and spend Christmas there. The children waited at the station for several hours, until a railroad employee took them aside and told them about the accident.

Adele Bongiovanni. *Reprint from* Gazette Times, *December 25, 1917.*

Adele Bongiovanni, age forty-two, was the wife of Frank Bongiovanni, the proprietor of the Nixon Café, a popular downtown restaurant and entertainment spot at 425 Sixth Avenue. Adele emigrated from Italy in 1905. She and her husband worked at the café prior to their marriage in 1910; they later acquired the business. She was on her way to the restaurant when the accident occurred. Adele sustained head lacerations and multiple broken bones and later died of pneumonia. After arriving at the hospital, the loss of her pocketbook containing several diamond rings and other jewelry worth about $2,000 and several hundred dollars was reported to the police. In the years before the accident, Adele and Frank Bongiovanni became generally well known in the Pittsburgh area through newspaper coverage of court actions related to their domestic discord.

The troubling sight of a young woman with a bloodied head, ragged fingernails and rumpled clothing wandering aimlessly for several hours through the aisles of a downtown department store on Christmas Eve aroused the curiosity of shoppers and the store detective. The detective said the woman appeared dazed. He approached her with care and asked if there was something wrong. The woman initially reacted with alarm but

Trio of Car Wreck Injured

Mrs E F De Martini

William Fleming

John P O'Malley

Plenty of Flour For Five Months

Though Exports Increase 50 Per Cent, Says Official, Nation Won't Suffer

City Detective Painfully Hurt, Does Rescue Work

Charles Freeborn.

Top, left: John P. O'Malley, William Fleming and Etra DeMartini. *Reprint from* Pittsburg Dispatch, *December 25, 1917.*

Top, right: Pittsburgh City detective Charles Freeborn, although hurt in the accident, worked to rescue fellow passengers until he fainted from his injuries and collapsed onto the street. *Reprint* Gazette Times, *December 25, 1917.*

KNOXVILLE MAN WHO WAS INJURED IN STREET CAR ACCIDENT AT TUNNEL

J. P. Gaede.

OLICEMAN CARRYING PRESENTS TO RELATIVES WAS VICTIM OF WRECK

James E. Cosgrove.

Bottom, left: Knoxville resident Reverend John P. Gaede was injured in the trolley accident. He was the minister at the First Seventh-day Adventist church in the Lincoln-Larimer area of the city. *Reprint from* Gazette Times, *December 25, 1917.*

Bottom, right: Pittsburgh police patrolman James F. Cosgrove, Beltzhoover, died in the trolley disaster. Well-known throughout the city, Cosgrove was assigned to the Oakland police station. *Reprint from* Gazette Times, *December 27, 1917.*

then became calm and somewhat embarrassed as she explained that after the trolley accident, she had fainted. When she came to, a stranger helped her from the car and onto another streetcar, and she continued downtown. The detective then called a cab to take her home. The woman, **Dorothy Lafferty**, age nineteen, of 203 Kingsboro Street, was the wife of *Pittsburgh Post* newspaperman C. Bruce Lafferty.

CHILDREN LEFT BEHIND

One of the saddest truths about the disaster was the high proportion of women among those who were killed or seriously injured. Women traveling downtown for last-minute holiday meal items or gifts were prominent among the passengers. While the exact number of children affected by the death or injury of their mothers is not known, a sense of the impact, particularly on very young children, can be seen by reading news articles from the days following the accident.

W.J. Byers from 419 Miller Street, Knoxville, shielded his three-year-old son, **Robert Byers**, from things that he couldn't comprehend. Surrounded by his Christmas toys, Robert kept asking for his mother. He didn't know that his mother was in South Side Hospital. His father told him she would be home as soon as she finished her shopping. Late on Christmas Day, the little boy rubbed his eyes as he whispered, "Tell my mother I waited all day for her, but I was too sleepy."

Grace, age three, and **William Duvall**, age two, played with a few Christmas toys on the parlor floor of the family home in Knoxville. The children were too young to realize that their mother, Sadie Duvall, age twenty-nine, lay in critical condition at St. Joseph's Hospital. A tree stood untrimmed on the rear porch. Sadie had been on her way to the city to finish Christmas shopping.

Calvin Brecht, age two, awoke on Christmas Day and found no tree or presents at his Knoxville home. His mother, Mabel F. Brecht, had so well hidden the gifts she bought for Calvin; his sister, Florence, age ten; and brother, Byron, age seven, that even the adults in the family could not find them. As Calvin cried repeatedly for his "mamma," his aunt, Lou Bennett, tried unsuccessfully to comfort him and the two older children over the death of their mother.

Laura Ohl's son, **Edward Jr.**, age six, escaped injury when he chose to stay at his Knoxville home to play with his cousins, Philip F., age ten, and Edward A. Miller, age twelve, rather than go into town with his mother. The Miller boys were visiting the Ohl home with their mother, Celia. Laura was seriously injured in the accident.

In a darkened room at 604 Lillian Street, Knoxville, lay the body of Rose M. Zurlinden. Among the heartbroken grandchildren were Grace Herrington, age six, and Martha Zurlinden, age seven. They stood dazed and sobbing. The trolley accident had taken their loving grandmother and companion. Rose had been on her way downtown to buy Christmas gifts for the little ones.

Three Women Victims of Horror

Mrs Mabel E Brecht   Miss Caroline M Fischer   Mrs Ella Sheridan

Mabel Brecht, Caroline Fischer and Ella Sheridan. *Reprint from* Pittsburg Dispatch, *December 26, 1917.*

The Christmas Eve tragedy intersected with the war effort for the Henry Klinzing family of 610 Delmont Avenue, Beltzhoover. While Henry stayed at home to set up the Christmas tree, his wife, **Mathilda**, went downtown to finish her shopping. Mathilda, the stepmother of four, Harry, Walter, Herman and Caroline, and mother of three, Mary, Helen and Joseph, died at the scene of the accident. Harry W. Klinzing, age twenty-two, the oldest of the Klinzing children, drafted into the army in September 1917, was among the first group from the Pittsburgh area to report to Fort Lee, Virginia, for training.

The *Pittsburg Post* on Christmas Day wrote about several who assisted with the rescue and care of the victims.

Smithfield Confectionary store employee **Robert Satler**, age sixteen, was likely the closest eyewitness to the accident. Satler was tending the peanut roaster just outside the front of the store at the corner of Carson and Smithfield Streets. As he turned to go back into the shop, he saw the car come rushing out of the tunnel. Satler narrowly escaped the catastrophe when the car toppled over and slid down the street, stopping only a few feet in front of him.

C.L.H. Smith, a traveling salesman from Wheeling, West Virginia, was waiting for a streetcar near the tunnel at Carson Street. He "heard a loud noise and shrieking" and then saw the Knoxville trolley running wild through the tunnel toward the city. At the front of the car, Smith saw the motorman frantically working to control the car while women and children fearfully clung to each other. When the car slid into the iron pole, the trolley split in half. As it tipped over, the roof on the rear end of the car hit a wooden pole. The wooden pole cut diagonally through the car. The front trucks stayed on the tracks and rolled about one hundred feet down Smithfield Street and crashed into a railing in front of the freight office, while the rear trucks, still attached to the car, landed near the door of the confectionery store. Passengers lay scattered across the streets and sidewalks or trapped inside the car's wreckage. Smith and Satler were the first to reach the wreckage. They moved the victims who were easiest to reach into the Smithfield Confectionary store and administered first aid.

J.D. Trefall, a freight agent for the P&LE Railroad, shortly after 3:00 p.m. was standing at a window on the first floor of the depot on the Carson Street side, talking with several of his clerks. Trefall, echoing Robert Satler's account, said he "heard a terrible rumbling just like the hill was coming in. Glancing out of the window, [he] saw the car coming wildly down the street on the opposite track. It crashed into a pole and carried the pole and portions of a small peanut stand on the corner with it in its flight. The front trucks of the car held on the track, but the rear ones and the body of the car turned over and over until it crashed into the railing of the [terminal annex] building." Trefall immediately telephoned for assistance and requested the operator summon every available ambulance, doctor and police surgeon in the city to the scene. He then directed all employees to assist in the rescue and hurried from the building, where he found "women and children were shrieking and parts of legs, heads, hair and feet were scattered on the grass and on the pavement beside the car. The scene was sickening and I was stunned."

Many of the dead and injured were moved into temporary morgues and hospitals set up in the P&LE Freight Annex and Birmingham Station. Trefall and his men, using all available first aid supplies in the building, cared for more than fifty of the injured before doctors arrived at the scene.

News reports also noted that William Smith Jr., a bystander from Munhall, and Frank D. Rogers, a PL&E Railroad accountant and Mount Washington resident, helped with the rescue.

Later, Satler described how terrible it was to hear the screams of passengers trapped in the wreckage as they waited to be removed from the car. Sadly, he said, "some of the dead were unrecognizable from their injuries." Satler believed he had put his Schenley High School first aid training to good use.

The son of Francis and Florence Satler of 3924 Mifflin Street, Lawrenceville, was the oldest of four children.

Smith helped with the rescue until he was overcome and was forced to leave. Prior to the accident, Smith was on his way to see his mother and sister in Beltzhoover.

A black cloud had certainly descended over Pittsburgh and the whole city grieved.

3

NEIGHBORHOOD INDIGNATION

*Indignation—anger, outrage, exasperation about a situation
that you think is wrong or unfair.*

MOUNTING TENSIONS

Differences between the public and the Pittsburgh Railways Co. intensified
after 1914, when the growth in population and increased war production
employment created greater demands for reliable streetcar service in and
out of the city during critical times of the day. Morning and evening rush
hours were especially troublesome when cars didn't run on schedule and
stops were often missed. Such inconsistency subjected workers and shoppers
to long waits at car stops and frequent overcrowding on the cars.

The Pittsburgh Railways Co. was ill-equipped to deal with the increase
in passenger volume. By expanding its system to less populated, outlying
areas to encourage residential development, the company operated almost
empty cars on some lines. War-related labor shortages forced the Pittsburgh
Railways Co. to take two hundred streetcars out of service. The company's
high proportion of inexperienced motormen, conductors and maintenance
personnel also contributed to service inefficiencies.

The December 22, 1917 announcement of a fare increase provoked
skepticism and outrage across the region, as well as threats by municipal
officials to take legal action and intervene in whatever way possible to
prevent the increase from going into effect.

Reaction to the Pittsburgh Railways fare increase was swift and strong. *Pittsburg Press, December 22, 1917.*

BREAKING POINT

The Mount Washington Tunnel accident was the breaking point for the citizens served by the Pittsburgh Railways Co., as well as the public officials, civic, business and trade organizations in the city and neighboring communities. In the accident's aftermath, overwhelming grief due to the substantial loss of life and scores of injuries, as well as a strong sense of indignation, spread throughout the area. Knoxville Borough quickly emerged as the epicenter for actions initiated in the days following the tragedy.

KNOXVILLE BOROUGH—EMOTIONALLY CHARGED ACTIONS

Knoxville's Borough Council and the Owners' and Renters' League both met at the King School on December 26, 1917, to develop strategies and "fix the blame for the tunnel disaster." Before the meetings, Burgess William Grimes acknowledged that Knoxville's grief was keenly felt, and the citizens would not rest until the crash had been thoroughly investigated and the responsible parties identified.

The council authorized its president, G.S. Larimar, and solicitor, W.D. Grimes, to request assistance from state and local officials. In a telegram to Governor Martin Brumbaugh, they asserted that the Pittsburgh Railways Co. was using the war as an excuse to endanger the lives and health of local residents and called for the Pennsylvania Public Service Commission to immediately take charge of the Pittsburgh Railways system to protect lives and prevent further tragedy. They requested the mobilization of the state police to prevent overcrowding and the county health department to ensure the cleaning and disinfecting of cars and recommended Attorney General Francis Brown revoke the Pittsburgh Railways Co.'s franchise agreements and prosecute the company for the accident.

Local officials, in their message, also recognized ongoing public discontent: "We call your attention to the fact that riots are of daily occurrence, streetcars are held up on the street, motorman are attacked, men, women and children are trampled and almost suffocated, men ride on the tops of cars, accidents are of frequent occurrence and the law is being violated and ridiculed by the officers and directors of the Pittsburgh Railways Company."

In a letter to Pittsburgh mayor Joseph G. Armstrong, Larimer insisted drastic measures be taken to abate the nuisance posed by the Pittsburgh Railways Co. and sought the city's support for the takeover of the transit system and operating it publicly or transferring it to someone who would more responsibly serve its patrons.

Solicitor Grimes requested that Allegheny County district attorney R.H. Jackson authorize county detectives and sheriff's deputies to arrest motormen and conductors who permitted crowding of the cars and asked for a grand jury investigation of the accident. In a letter to Coroner Jamison, Grimes argued for the arrest of Pittsburgh Railways Co. officials on manslaughter charges, carelessness and negligence and urged that the case against railway officials not be "whitewashed."

Three days after the accident, on December 27, when Coroner Jamison failed to act, Grimes announced that Knoxville Council intended to swear out arrest warrants charging every Pittsburgh Railways Co. official with manslaughter. He claimed the entire borough supported this action and would not stand idly by and allow the transit company to deflect blame onto the motorman.

Local monitoring of the street rail system increased when Knoxville Council authorized the appointment of twenty men to the borough's health department. The officers, posted at various points along the Knoxville car route, were to ensure that streetcars were kept sanitary, were not overcrowded and that schedules were maintained. The agents could also arrest motormen and conductors who were in violation of local regulations. The agents worked in conjunction with the Knoxville Owners' and Renters' League. Borough officials urged other municipalities to take similar action to inspect all cars entering their communities.

NEIGHBORING COMMUNITIES

Officials of neighboring communities acted quickly to issue declarations in support of Knoxville Borough and its 5,800 residents. Among the first were Carrick and Brentwood, boroughs just south of Knoxville. Carrick, in addition to expressing sorrow and sincere sympathy to those who lost loved ones and wishes for a speedy recovery to the injured, pledged its intent "to cooperate with any bodies striving to prevent a repetition of such an accident and to improve conditions in general that place loved ones in jeopardy." Brentwood echoed Carrick's sentiments and added that its borough's solicitor would "render assistance to better transit conditions and safeguard the lives of the citizens of our community."

FIRST CITIZEN COMMENTS

Helen Grimes, Knoxville resident and president of the Congress of Western PA Women's Clubs, was one of the first to speak out. She told of her recent experiences with cars dashing through the Mount Washington Tunnel at full speed as motormen tried to make up time and her fear that an accident like the one on Christmas Eve would happen. Grimes recalled the Mount Washington Tunnel accident in January 1905, less than two months after the tunnel opened. It and the Christmas Eve tragedy were strikingly similar. The *Pittsburg Press* on January 16, 1905, reported that six of the seventy-five passengers on an inbound Pittsburgh Railways Co. trolley suffered injuries requiring hospitalization, when about halfway through the tunnel a fuse blew out and disabled the car's brakes. According to passenger Charles Nolte of Beltzhoover, the car was packed to suffocation with people crowding the aisles and rear platform. The car was careening through the tunnel at a high rate of speed when something snapped. The car "shot forward with lightning speed" as the "motorman excitedly worked the brakes."

Details of the 1905 accident reported by the *Pittsburg Press* were strikingly similar to the December 24, 1917 accident. The *Pittsburg Press* article indicated that the car remained on the track as it emerged from the tunnel. When the trolley hit the curve between the tunnel and Carson Street, it jumped from the inbound track, over the outbound track and then turned sideways as it bounced twenty-five feet across the cobblestones onto Carson Street. After the car turned sideways, it crashed into an iron trolley and a wooden telegraph pole at the northwest corner of Carson and Smithfield Streets. The impact tore the rear platform and trucks from the car and threw everyone on the back of the car onto the street. The car turned again and was dragged up Smithfield Street for several feet. Bystanders, expecting the worst, rushed to the scene to render assistance.

Knoxville Owners' and Renters' League— Tempered Reactions

Over two hundred people attended the first mass meeting of the Knoxville Owners' and Renters' League on December 26, 1917. After much discussion, the crowd pledged to operate as a unified group to prevent a recurrence of the tunnel accident. The league formed two committees: one to focus on presenting testimony to the Pennsylvania Public Service Commission about improving streetcar service, preventing accidents and investigating the legality of the pending fare increase and the other to visit the homes of the grief-stricken and injured.

At the end of the league's meeting, Solicitor Grimes reported on the actions authorized by Knoxville Borough Council. League president C. Lawrence Cook called the borough's decisions drastic and insisted that it was not the time for fireworks or hasty actions. Instead, he counseled, cooler heads must prevail. The league's car service committee chair, S.J. Snee, stated that a business approach combined with civil actions would be more successful in securing better and safer transit. Snee added that the city's help in seeking changes was essential since Knoxville alone was helpless.

By December 29, Knoxville burgess William Grimm and S.N. Snee, on behalf of the Knoxville Owners' and Renters' League, and Pittsburgh mayor J.G. Armstrong jointly petitioned the governor and Pennsylvania Public

Service Commission to convene a Pittsburgh-based investigative hearing on streetcar safety issues and the fare increase.

On January 3, 1918, the outgoing Knoxville Borough Council deferred action against Pittsburgh Railways Co. officials until after the county finished its accident investigation. Coroner Jamison, on December 27, had charged the Knoxville trolley motorman with manslaughter and the dispatcher as an accessory to manslaughter. In addition, District Attorney Jackson was considering having a grand jury investigate the accident. Determining whether there was a need for further action was left to Knoxville's newly elected officials who would take office the next week. A majority of the new council were members of the Knoxville Owners' and Renters' League and had previously committed to fight on behalf of Knoxville's residents.

The Knoxville Owners' and Renters' League and the South Hills Union for Better Car Service held several joint mass meetings in January 1918. Those who attended believed cooperating with state and local governments would force the Pittsburgh Railways Co. to improve street railway conditions. They recommended the county create a streetcar inspection bureau and impose a requirement that cars going through the tunnel must test their brakes by coming to a full stop upon entering the tunnel. The group was also concerned about the prospect of losing federal war production contracts due to unreliable car service and the possibility that the Pittsburgh Railways Co.'s financial instability would soon force the company into receivership.

Similar mass meetings to protest the fare increase and demand safer transit occurred across Allegheny County. Residents and businesses in Mount Washington, Allentown, Mount Oliver, Beltzhoover, Dormont, Carrick, St. Clair, Bellevue and Wilkinsburg pledged moral and financial support to the Knoxville Owners' and Renters' League. Public support was expected to grow throughout the Pittsburgh Railways Co. service area. The South Hills Union for Better Car Service echoed the Knoxville Council's concern over the intensity of the public's discontent when it warned that public patience was at a breaking point when it called on Allegheny County sheriff William S. Haddock to use his power to prevent car fare increases and quell any public disorder that may cause bodily harm and destruction of property, if an increase went into effect.

PENNSYLVANIA PUBLIC SERVICE COMMISSION HEARING

On January 17, 1918, Pennsylvania's Public Service Commission chairman, W.D.B. Ainey, convened a hearing in Pittsburgh to take testimony on car service issues. Representatives of four large local plants including Westinghouse Electric, East Pittsburgh, using records of inconsistent employee arrival times, demonstrated how the absence of reliable car service for their workers affected war production and warned that interference would result in lost lives on the battlefield. Twenty-six thousand complaints gathered from members of the Commercial Club, its forty constituent groups and the general public were presented by J. Ralph Park as evidence of the car service problem. The balance of the hearing focused on the commission's October 16, 1917 order requiring the Pittsburgh Railways Co. to restore to service two hundred cars the company previously removed from the schedule due to bad weather and insufficient personnel to operate the cars. Chairman Ainey confirmed that a fine of $50 per car per day, plus penalties, beginning on December 22, was still in force and the accumulated fine already totaled $400,000. Pittsburgh Railways Co. president S.L. Tone testified that the company could not restore the two hundred cars to service and contended that current service was adequate under wartime conditions. Tone also threatened the breakup of the company if the fare increase did not go into effect. In response to criticism that stockholders of the seventy-five underlying transit companies made money at the expense of the passengers, C.S. Mitchell, the company's controller, acknowledged that about $2.1 million of a $12 million operating budget was paid each year in dividends to Pittsburgh Railways Co. stockholders.

In mid-January, the Public Service Commission reported that John P. Dohoney, the commission's head investigator, found overcrowding and carelessness, rather than brake failure, caused the Mount Washington Tunnel accident. With this announcement, two paths emerged—one followed the criminal prosecution of the motorman and conductor and the other focused on the fight against the fare increase and the continuing struggle for adequate, reliable and safe street transit service by local officials, civic groups and the public.

On January 22, the day the fare increase was to go into effect, Allegheny County Common Pleas Court judge John D. Shafer denied a petition by six municipalities to stop it. In his order, Shafer stated the responsibility for such decisions rested with the Pennsylvania Public Service Commission, not the courts. That same day, a news reporter asked patrons waiting at bus stops about the fare increase. The universal response was "I don't mind the extra money—if they'd only give us service."

CITY TAKES THE LEAD

Coincidental to the court's decision, Pittsburgh newly elected mayor, Edward V. Babcock, appointed a six-member Industrial Transportation Committee to work with the state's Public Service Commission to identify ways to make the street rail system more efficient and effective. This constituted a first step in taking the lead on behalf of the public's interest. The committee members included John W. Weibly, president of Pittsburgh Taxicab Co.; Reid Kennedy, president of the Monongahela Trust Co.; J.B. Rider, vice president of Pressed Steel Car Co.; David J. Berry, managing editor of the *National Labor Journal*; A.N.W. Robertson, attorney for the Pittsburgh Railways Co.; and David C. Ainey, assistant engineer for the Pennsylvania Public Service Commission. The group was to rely on reports of the city's transit commissioner and the Public Service Commission, as well as testimony from commercial and industrial concerns to find ways to encourage greater general ridership and shopping in off hours, alleviate war production problems caused by unreliable street transit schedules and solicit the cooperation of municipal, business, trade and civic groups in problem-solving.

FRAGILE TIMES—PUBLIC FEAR AND INDIGNATION

Local residents who relied on the Pittsburgh Railways Co. for transportation faced two realities. Streetcar transit was inherently unsafe. And streetcar travel was essentially unreliable. Public fear and indignation intensified in the weeks following the Christmas Eve tragedy as over half a dozen panic-inducing trolley incidents were reported. At the same time, rising anger drove extraordinary actions when some chose to take matters into their own hands, giving credence to the warnings issued by municipal officials and civic leaders. The neighborhood response would not be complete without including more specific discussion of trolley incidents and acts of public indignation.

CORONER CONCERNED

Concern for streetcar passenger safety was seen as early as 1913 in the Allegheny County Coroner's annual report of death investigations.

Coroner Jamison warned that streetcar-related fatalities had increased by 26 percent over the prior year. He stated that 56 lives had been lost in streetcar accidents despite "consistent efforts to educate the public to a proper appreciation of the dangers of carelessness" and pleading with "those descending from street cars and pedestrians at street crossings to remain on the curb line until the car has passed to avoid stepping in front of some vehicle which has been concealed from view by the car." Subsequent years' news coverage of the coroner's activities did not report fatalities on a categorical basis but did indicate that violent deaths climbed from 3,177 in 1913 to 3,627 in 1917, exclusive of those who died in the Mount Washington trolley accident, and lamented the continuing absence of measures that would safeguard the public on highways and street crossings. It's unlikely that the number of streetcar accidents that resulted in death or injury did not continue as a concern. The indices of the Allegheny County Courts–Civil Division over these same years are filled with dozens of civil suits filed against the Pittsburgh Railways Co. by private individuals, which provide further affirmation of the frequency of incidents involving streetcars and passengers or pedestrians.

INCIDENTS STOKE FEAR

The tunnel accident acted as the "tipping point" for the public. In the weeks following the Christmas Eve accident, at least seven incidents involving Pittsburgh Railways Co. streetcars were reported by the local press, with three, noted below, occurring on December 27, three days after the trolley disaster.

"Another Crowded Car Jumps Track": A defective track switch caused a crowded inbound car to jump the tracks at West Liberty and Warrington Avenues at 9:00 a.m. on December 27. Although no one was injured, the accident caused considerable excitement. Some of the women suffered from shock and the motorman was scratched by flying glass.

"Repetition of Xmas Eve Wreck on 44 Car, Nearly Averted": A repeat of the Christmas Eve trolley tragedy was narrowly averted on December 27, just before 6:00 p.m. when the air brake of Knoxville car No. 44 failed to operate. The car loaded with homebound travelers stopped after speeding about two blocks down Beltzhoover Avenue from Warrington to Climax Street. The car stopped when it started up the steep grade after passing Climax Street. No one was injured, and the car did not leave the track.

About eighty passengers were shifted to another car when the motorman refused to operate the trolley.

"Streetcar Ignites; Crowd Is in a Panic": Men, women and children on West Park Car No. 3205 were panic-stricken when flames burst through the car floor as it approached Locust Street and Chartiers Avenue in McKees Rocks. The fire broke out after the car left the track near the West End car barn. No injuries were reported, although many women's dresses were scorched.

Less than a week later, on January 3, 1918, two more incidents were reported.

"Passengers in Panic When Car Ignites": Panic ensued as passengers rushed to the exits in the evening on an outbound Negley Avenue car when it erupted into flames at Twenty-Fifth Street and Penn Avenue. Passengers on the car saw smoke and alerted the motorman, who put the fire out with a bucket of water from a nearby store.

"Car Strikes Wagon; Three Persons Hurt": Passengers were hurled to the floor when the brakes on a Duquesne streetcar failed as it descended the hill at the Thompson Bridge shortly before noon on January 3. The trolley struck a Deer Coal Company wagon. Three passengers sustained bruises, fractured legs, ribs and shoulders. Neither the truck driver nor the motorman was injured.

And perhaps the most harrowing experience reported came on January 11, 1918, for the passengers on Knoxville No. 4718.

"Knoxville Car Runs Wild on Steep Grade": An inbound Knoxville streetcar carrying more than one hundred passengers ran away on Beltzhoover Avenue at 9:00 a.m. on January 11. After the trolley left Orchard Place in Knoxville, it raced down the hill toward Climax Street in Beltzhoover and climbed up the steep grade from Climax Street to Warrington Avenue. Passengers on the packed Knoxville car panicked when the brakes failed and the car threatened to leave the tracks. Women screamed, and the men rushed toward the exits when the car came to a stop near Industry Street. As the men jumped and pushed their way off the car, the car moved backward down the grade toward Climax Street but was brought to a stop before it had gained any momentum.

Passengers confirmed that the motorman applied all the brakes as it started down the slope from Orchard Place, but none appeared to work. The motorman then shouted to the conductor to apply the emergency brake, but the conductor was too excited to do so. The steep hill to Warrington Avenue prevented the Knoxville car from running across Warrington Avenue and colliding with either the Arlington or Beltzhoover cars. The motorman, so new to the job that he didn't have a uniform, refused to take the car farther and vowed never to run another streetcar in Pittsburgh. Many passengers, frightened by the experience, refused transfer to other cars and walked into the city.

A passenger, Robert Risch of 444 Arabella Street, said that "only the encountering of a steep upgrade and Providence prevented a recurrence of the Christmas eve streetcar disaster."

"Three Big Cars in Smash": Over fifty inbound passengers were injured in a three-car collision on January 26 near the Fairhaven Station (Castle Shannon) at 4:30 p.m. The first Charleroi car stopped when its air brakes failed to operate, possibly due to a short circuit. The motorman of the second Charleroi car safely stopped his trolley and attempted to flag down a third car. The motorman of the Washington car, traveling about thirty miles per hour in blizzard conditions, could not see the flagman's red lantern until he was too close to the second car to stop, even though he applied his brakes and dropped sand on the snow-and-ice-covered tracks. The Washington car crashed into the rear of the second car and pushed it into the first car. Passengers were thrown against broken windows and onto the car floors.

PUBLIC INDIGNATION PROMPTS PUBLIC ACTION

Surging frustration among trolley patrons across the Pittsburgh area sparked acts of passenger insurrection in the weeks after the tunnel accident. The first occurred on December 25 at 11:50 p.m. when a crowd of two hundred waiting outbound passengers at Station Street and Franktown Avenue threw stones at the car and pulled the trolley from the wire when the motorman and conductor turned the outbound Lincoln Avenue car back into the city. A woman suffered a head injury when a stone crashed through a window.

One of the most dramatic incidents occurred when a Pittsburgh Railways dispatcher at the south end of the Mount Washington Tunnel refused a passenger's request to turn some empty outbound cars back toward the city. A cold and angry group of workers had walked from the Knoxville and the Mount Washington area to the tunnel's South Portal seeking a ride. The crowd of over three hundred stampeded to the tunnel after the young man whose request had been denied yelled, "C'mon, I'm going through the hole." Crowded cars moved slowing through the tunnel behind the throng of men, boys, women and girls as they walked through the tunnel in protest.

From Mount Washington Tunnel's opening in December 1904 until January 1918, no local resident had walked through it. By mid-January 1918, it had happened twice. The second incident occurred within a few days of the first, when about one hundred Beltzhoover men on their way to work on a Tuesday morning were "disgusted because of their inability to get transportation en route to the city" and walked through the Mount Washington Tunnel. The men waited from 7:00 a.m. to 8:10 a.m. at their stop and then walked through deep snow to the south end of the tunnel. Gathered at the South Portal were large crowds of people who had been unable to board cars at their regular stops. Cars from Beechview, Dormont, Mount Washington, Brookline and Charleroi were packed when they approached the tunnel. Only a few passengers could squeeze onto the cars. Several hundred people were left waiting as the cars disappeared into the tunnel. The men began to grumble. As the sentiments spread through the crowd, one man shouted, "Let's walk through this tube." He began to trudge through the snow to the tunnel, and many others followed.

Commandeering a car was dubbed "kidnapping" by the *Pittsburgh Post*. The paper reported an outbound Bloomfield and an outbound Brookline were kidnapped by impatient crowds waiting in downtown during the evening rush hour on January 11. The same ruse was used in both cases: "someone pulled the trolley off and everyone piled on." The Bloomfield car stopped at Fifth Avenue and Wood Street, but the conductor did not open the door. One of the would-be passengers stepped onto the rear of the car and pulled the trolley off. The conductor then had to open the door to replace the trolley, and the crowd scrambled onto the car.

After waiting an hour at Third Avenue between Smithfield and Wood Street, a crowd seized a Brookline trolley bound for the barn by rushing out in front of the car. When the conductor refused to open the door, someone pulled the trolley off and another pulled the door open, and everyone boarded. With a car packed full of people, the motorman returned to the barn and changed crews, and the journey to Brookline continued.

A last demonstration of frustration occurred on the Homeville line and was initiated by a group of young women. On the morning of January 15, seven young women were on their way to work in Homestead when the conductor told them to exit the car at the Munhall Junction about half a mile from their destination. The car was returning to Rankin car barn. The women refused to exit. The car turned around and headed to the barn with the women on board. At the West Braddock Bridge, the conductor again told them to leave the car. An argument erupted. One woman struck the conductor. When the others joined in, the conductor fled the scene. The women then attacked the motorman. He was able to lock himself in his cab and returned to the barn. At the barn, the women again argued with the motormen. The motormen returned the car to the Munhall Junction, where the women were threatened with arrest if they did not leave the car. They then left the car and walked to Homestead.

Ultimately, the City of Pittsburgh, as the grantor of operating franchises to the Pittsburgh Railways Co. for three hundred of the six-hundred-mile transit system, took the lead in representing the interests of the public and local governments in dealing with street railway issues. At the end of February 1918, as the company moved toward bankruptcy, the city had formally requested the federal court's permission to intervene in the legal proceedings to represent the public's interests.

4
FAMILY TIES

O nce I found that Aurelia Kuffner Czerny was a victim of the Mount Washington Tunnel disaster, I wanted to learn more about her and her family, their life in Pittsburgh and their connection to my grandparents. The Czerny family arrived in Allegheny County in 1909 from Valašské Meziříčí, a city in eastern Moravia, as part of a family chain migration process. Leopold, age forty, and his sons, Leopold Jr., age fifteen, and Theodore, age eleven, immigrated in August, and Aurelia, age thirty-four, and her daughters, Marie, age twelve, and Irene, age ten, arrived in December. My grandfather Johann D. Kuffner, age twenty-two, arrived in the United States in July 1910. His mother, Josefa (Josephine), age forty-five, and sister, Stefania (Stephanie), age seventeen, immigrated in April 1911. My grandmother Aloise Miksch was the last to emigrate, in April 1913. They came through the ports of Baltimore or New York and all cited Leetsdale, Pennsylvania, as their destination, with Fred (Ferdinand) Bauer as their sponsor. Fannie (Frances) Bauer, Fred's wife, was Grandpa's older sister. The Bauers came in 1907, at age twenty-five and twenty, and were sponsored by Anthony and Mary Bauer, Fred's brother and sister-in-law, who arrived in 1905. Like many others who immigrated from Austria-Hungary, the Bauer, Czerny and Kuffner families applied to become American citizens soon after they arrived in the United States.

Opportunities in Pittsburgh's glass industry drew the Czerny and Kuffner families to the city. By the early 1900s, Pittsburgh's location west of the Allegheny Mountains; the availability of sand, soda ash and lime; access to

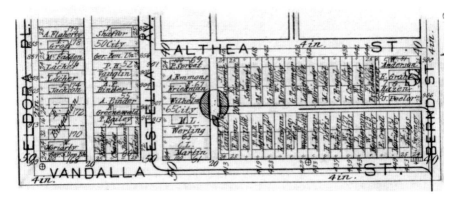

A 1916 Hopkins Map depicting Althea Street, Beltzhoover, the location of the Czerny Family residence. *Courtesy of Archives & Special Collections, University of Pittsburgh Library System.*

coal and gas for fuel; and the city's proximity to river transportation placed it in the heart of the southwestern Pennsylvania, West Virginia and Ohio glass production, where hundreds of factories produced 80 percent of the nation's pressed, blown and plate glass. On the city's South Side, glass factories, homes, businesses, churches and schools were packed into the space between Mount Washington and the Monongahela River. As skilled Bohemian tradesmen from glass-making areas of Moravia, both Leopold Czerny, a glass pattern maker, and John Kuffner, a glass blower, came seeking a better life.

In December 1917, the Czerny family lived in a two-story, six-room, insulbrick home on a twenty-five-foot-wide lot at 438 Althea Street in Beltzhoover. Five of their seven children still lived at home, including Leo Jr. and Theodore, a machinist and a mechanic, both at Westinghouse Electric in East Pittsburgh; Angeline, age seven; Alfred, age five; and Leona, age three. Two married daughters lived outside the city, Marie Horova in Detroit and Irene Walenta in Charleroi.

Official information about Aurelia's death is sparse. A report issued by St. Joseph's Hospital stated Aurelia Czerny, age forty-five, married and a housewife was "brought in dead." She died at 3:30 p.m. Under cause of death was "Pittsburgh Railways street car accident at Smithfield and Carson Street." The death certificate issued by the coroner indicated "entire body crushed due to streetcar wreck" and noted that it was "probably accidental." Services were conducted on December 28 at St. George's Catholic Church. She was buried at St. John Vianney Cemetery, Brownsville Road, Carrick. Her husband, Leo, confined to St. Joseph's Hospital, was unable to attend the funeral.

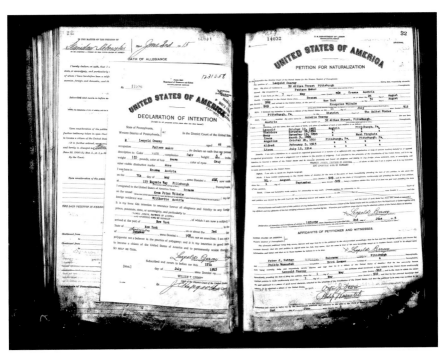

Leopold A. Czerny naturalization papers, September 14, 1915. *National Archives, Washington, D.C., Record Group Title: M1537.*

Aurelia Czerny grave, Saint John Vianney Cemetery, St. George Section, Pittsburgh. *Photo by author.*

Several newspaper articles published immediately after the wreck, when woven together, create an impression of the accident's impact on the Czerny family. One under the heading, "Tree Was Trimmed," described preparations in the home that were strikingly familiar to the experiences my brother, sister and I had as children forty years later.

The *Pittsburgh Post* reported that Mr. and Mrs. Leo Czerny of 438 Althea Street, Beltzhoover, had secretly trimmed the Christmas tree in a darkened room on the second floor of their home on Monday (Christmas Eve) and then started to the city to purchase toys for the three youngest children and gifts for the older children. The father and mother never returned from their trip to the city. The three little ones, left alone in the house, were quiet until long after the supper hour. When the next-door neighbor, Minnie Whitezell of 442 Althea Street, heard them sobbing, she took them to her home. A short time later, Minnie was informed of the accident. She cared for the children on Christmas Eve night and Christmas Day and said that the arrival of every visitor caused the children to rush to the door, still expecting to see Daddy and Mother coming home. Little Leona persistently asked, "Is my mama coming home?" Mrs. Whitezell added, "The children continually cry for their mother, and it is impossible to comfort them." She borrowed toys from neighbors, which distracted the children for a short time, until they again cried for their mama.

Following the disaster, crowds gathered at the accident scene, local hospitals and the Allegheny County morgue. Among the reports published on Christmas Eve was "Frantic Crowds Besiege Morgue and Hospitals, Boy Identifies Mother." It stated:

> *Perhaps the most pathetic case witnessed was that of Leo Czerny of 438 Althea Street, who followed a curious crowd into the morgue, only to find his mother's body among the dead.*
>
> *When young Czerny got a glimpse of his mother's dead face, he emitted a scream of grief that resounded throughout the building and cried pathetically as Matron McCullough and Deputy Coroner Hugh Dempsey assisted him into the retiring room, where he was given water and consoled. A morbid crowd followed the young man to the retiring room, and it required the efforts of the matron and deputy coroners to keep the curious people back.*

He then was informed by a friend that his father, Leo Czerny, lay in St. Joseph's Hospital, the sight of one eye perhaps destroyed, his shoulder broken and his head badly contused.

By 1920, the Czerny family was almost gone from Pittsburgh. Leo Sr. survived his injuries and was living in Detroit with his oldest daughter, Marie, and her husband, Anthony Horova. The youngest children, Angeline, Alfred and Leona, were also in Detroit living with Leo Jr. and his wife, Mary. Pennsylvania vital records indicate that in March 1927, Angeline, at age sixteen, passed away at Mercy Hospital. It appears that her father provided information for the death certificate and gave a Pittsburgh address. By the early 1930s, Leo Sr. was remarried and had moved to Lancaster, Ohio, where he worked as a glass mold maker for Stuck Mould Works. He later joined two of his children, Alfred Czerny and Leona Morrison, in Fairmont, West Virginia, and lived there until his death in 1949.

Of the seven children, only Theodore remained in the Pittsburgh area. He married in 1938. He and his wife, Gertrude (Zende), and their son, Theodore Jr., and daughters, Doris, Virginia and Annabelle, lived in Wilkinsburg. Sometime after 1942, Theodore and Gertrude Czerny moved to Steubenville, Ohio. And, from existing records, it appears that Annabelle Czerny Perryman and her family, husband, J. Edwin, and sons, James E. and Randall E., were the last links to Aurelia in the Pittsburgh area. Annabelle Perryman lived in Forest Hills, Pennsylvania, until 2007.

PART II

THE BACK STORY

5

BUILDING THE
MOUNT WASHINGTON TUNNEL

Introduction

On December 1, 1904, when the first streetcar carrying passengers passed through the Mount Washington Tunnel at 5:05 a.m., the tunnel became the longest street railway tunnel in the world. The tunnel, proposed fifty years earlier, was indeed a reality. It took slightly more than two years to bore through the mountain called Coal Hill on the western side of the Monongahela River, near where it merges with the Allegheny River to form the mighty Ohio River. An early 1820s letter by traveling Scotsman James Flint described Mount Washington as "a craggy steep almost close to the river…covered by trees to the summit and tends more than any other object to give Pittsburg a picturesque appearance." Local trolley routes traversing the hillside provided passengers with superbly spectacular views as they leaped over rivers and ravines, plunged through woods and climbed over and through the western foothills of the Appalachian Mountains.

For more than one hundred years, the hillside acted as a barrier to travel in and out of Pittsburgh from southern Allegheny County and Washington County. The tunnel eliminated the previous circuitous route and shortened travel time 75 to 80 percent, from forty-five to sixty minutes to ten to twelve minutes, depending on the time of day.

View of Mount Washington hillside prior to construction of the tunnel, with the Castle Shannon Incline on the left side and the Mount Washington Incline on the right. Smithfield Street Bridge over the Monongahela River at lower right. *Courtesy of Carnegie Library of Pittsburgh, Pennsylvania Department, Photograph Collection.*

By 1901, the Mount Washington Street Railway Co., Mount Washington Tunnel Co. and Beechwood Development Co. (also known as the Pittsburg Tunnel Co.) proposed dueling tunnels with North Portals about six and a half feet apart. Both tunnels would run through Mount Washington from the South Hills Junction at Warrington Avenue in Beltzhoover to the intersection of Carson and Smithfield Streets. From there, trolley riders could access railway service to locations in the eastern United States from the Pittsburgh & Lake Erie Station or continue across the Smithfield Street Bridge to downtown Pittsburgh.

The Smithfield Street Bridge had served as a critical north–south Monongahela River crossing point since the early 1800s. The bridge, designed by Gustav Lindenthal, has a lenticular, or lens-shaped, truss structure. From its opening in 1883 to 1911, as the volume of traffic increased, the bridge underwent multiple expansions from two to three and ultimately four lanes to accommodate streetcar, horse-drawn wagon, motor vehicle and pedestrian traffic.

View from North Portal of the Mount Washington Tunnel toward the Smithfield Street Bridge at Carson and Smithfield Streets, 1911. *Courtesy of Archives & Special Collections, University of Pittsburgh Library System.*

CONFLICT AMONG COMPETITORS

Both tunnel companies obtained charters from the Commonwealth of Pennsylvania to bore passages through Mount Washington. The Pittsburg Tunnel Co. was chartered on April 30, 1897, to construct, maintain and operate a 3,750-foot-long tunnel from the intersection of Sycamore and Carson Streets to a point in the Bailey Estate. The Beechwood Development Co., headed by a former state senator, William Flinn, expecting that the tunnel's quicker access to the city would trigger significant housing growth beyond the northern end of Mount Washington and into the southern suburbs, invested $500,000 in the construction of residential roads and sewers.

About four and a half years later, on October 15, 1901, the state granted a charter to the Mount Washington Tunnel Co. to construct, maintain and operate a tunnel in the city of Pittsburgh, from Sycamore and Carson Streets to the Chess Street area. In early 1902, the Mount Washington Tunnel Co. obtained approval for a route change. The tunnel would run from Carson Street in a straight line south through lots 63, 21 and 22 in the S.L. Boggs Plan in Pittsburgh's Thirty-Second Ward.

The state grant of charters for tunnels through Mount Washington along essentially the same route, with northern portals six and a half feet apart, set the stage for a legal battle. In March 1902, the Mount Washington Tunnel Co. sued the Pittsburg Tunnel Co. in the Allegheny County Court of Common Pleas to obtain the exclusive right to construct a tunnel. The company alleged that the lack of progress shown by the Pittsburg Tunnel Co. after it awarded a $500,000 contract to John Nicholson Jr. in April 1899 indicated that it had no intention of completing the project. The Pittsburg Tunnel Co. countered by requesting that the court extend its five-year charter, which the Mount Washington Tunnel Co. opposed. Common Pleas Court No. 1 judge E.S. Stowe heard the case in April 1902.

On June 3, 1902, Booth and Flinn Ltd., a bridge and tunnel construction company founded by William Flinn, began work on behalf of the Mount Washington Tunnel Co. By June 5, 1902, Booth and Flinn alleged that the Pittsburgh Tunnel Co. was interfering with its work and requested that city police stand guard to prevent potential violence between competing tunnel crews. Less than two weeks later, on June 17, the Pittsburg Tunnel Co. offered to buy out Booth and Flinn and the Mount Washington Tunnel Co. for expenses incurred for materials and labor to date. In response, Booth and Flinn accelerated its work by creating a two-tent encampment on the side of the hill to permit crews split into day and night shifts to work twenty-four hours per day. As the Mount Washington Tunnel Co. workers proceeded to shear off the hillside, there was no action at the Pittsburg Tunnel Co. site. (Note that William Flinn, as an owner of the Beechwood Development Co. and founder of Booth and Flinn, was involved in both sides of this conflict.)

On June 25, 1902, Judge Stowe ruled that both tunnels could be built since both had valid charters and should not be impeded in their efforts.

Meanwhile, the Mount Washington Tunnel Co. continued to make progress and generate complaints. Rocks and mud flowed onto Sycamore Street. Middle-of-the-night dynamite blasts kept Mount Washington residents awake. On July 13, 1902, the Pittsburgh, Cincinnati & St. Louis Railroad, claiming risk to people and property, sued the Mount Washington Tunnel Co. when blasting at the north entrance to the tunnel hurled rocks onto its tracks and station.

Three months later, on September 1, 1902, the Pittsburg Tunnel Co. began work on its tunnel. By September 9, 1902, the company had alleged that blasting by the Mount Washington Tunnel Co. had damaged the Pittsburg Tunnel Company's construction site.

LABORERS SERENELY CAMP IN A PERILOUS LOCATION

High up on the side of Mt. Washington two tents are pitched in niches in the rocks. There is a margin of but a few feet of space on the shelf where the tents rest, and yet, like cliff dwellers, a gang of Italian laborers sleep beneath the canvas as if they were in as perfect security as in a house in the city proper.

A fight between contractors resulted in the pitching of the tents on dangerous ground, so that the men engaged on the work could watch at all times lest their rivals steal a march on them.

The work in progress is the drilling of a tunnel through Mt. Washington, entering the hillside opposite the south end of the Smithfield street bridge. Some years ago John Nicholson, a contractor, acquired the right of way to dig beneath the property, which was owned by John Auth, a pioneer on Mt. Washington. Work was started on the tunnel, but only in a small way, and but little progress was made in a number of years. Recently a new company was organized to drill a tunnel through Mt. Washington, and rights were secured to the same piece of property. Then the trouble began.

Booth & Flinn, the contractors for the new company, placed 25 laborers on the hillside to cut a facing for the tunnel. Men in Nicholson's employ attempted to dig on the top of the hill and roll the loosened earth into the works of the gang half way down the hill. In order to prevent this, Booth & Flinn's men pitched two tents on the precipitous height and remained there night and day. Should they roll through the tent in their sleep they would be dashed to death on the rocks far below. It is a queer camping place.

During the height of the tunnel controversy, Booth and Flinn, the contractor for the Mount Washington Tunnel Co., housed workmen on the site in two tents precariously perched on the rocky hillside to protect the worksite from vandalism by competing Pittsburg Tunnel Co. employees. *Reprint from* Pittsburg Press, *June 22, 1902.*

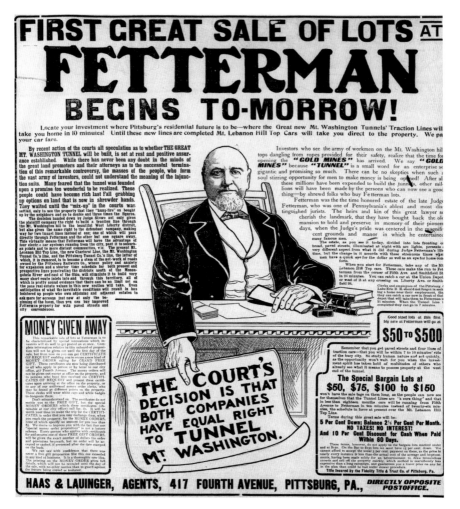

Above: Residential lots for sale. The opening of the Mount Washington Tunnel was expected to greatly reduce travel time for those who wanted to live in the suburbs south of the city. *Reprint from* Pittsburg Press, *September 13, 1902.*

Opposite, top: The Pittsburgh Railways tunnel route under the streets of Mount Washington is shown from the South Portal at Warrington Avenue to the North Portal at Carson and Smithfield Streets. A slight curve in the tunnel was located beneath Tuscola Street. *1910 Atlas of Greater Pittsburgh, Plate 30, Courtesy of Archives & Special Collections, University of Pittsburgh Library System.*

Opposite, bottom: Pittsburgh Railways Co. Series #4200 car exiting Mount Washington Tunnel at North Portal at Smithfield and Carson Streets. *Courtesy of* Pittsburgh Post-Gazette.

Above: The South Portal of the Mount Washington Tunnel at Warrington Avenue. *Courtesy of Archives & Special Collections, University of Pittsburgh Library System.*

Opposite, top: Passengers boarding Mount Washington streetcar at the South Hills Junction stop, June 1916. *Courtesy of Courtesy of Archives & Special Collections, University of Pittsburgh Library System.*

Opposite, bottom: Workers at northern entrance to Mount Washington Tunnel at Sycamore Street. Sycamore Street was displaced as a result of the construction. *Reprint from* Pittsburgh Weekly Gazette, *December 5, 1902.*

On January 17, 1903, the Pittsburg Tunnel Co. amended its earlier suit against the Mount Washington Tunnel Co. and Booth and Flinn to include damages to its construction site caused by work on the Mount Washington Tunnel Co. project.

Newspaper coverage about the tunnel conflict essentially ceased until June 5, 1903. On that day came the announcement that the Philadelphia Company had purchased $2 million in bonds issued by the Mount

TUNNEL WHICH WM. FLINN'S COMPANY IS CUTTING INTO MT. WASHINGTON
(Photographed for The Gazette.)

Entrance to Tunnel at Head of
Sycamore Street.

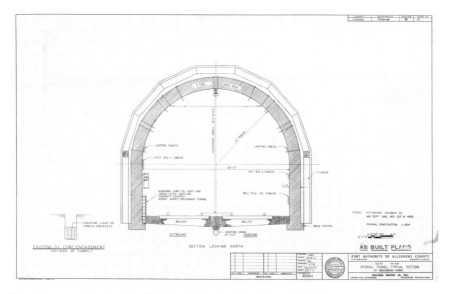

Tunnel construction drawing. The South Portal of the Mount Washington tunnel is depicted. Looking northward into the tunnel, details drawn from the 1904 Pittsburgh Railways construction plans show the timbers that frame the tunnel interior, the horseshoe-shaped concrete and the brick tunnel walls and ceiling, the depth of the interior footers, north and south bound tracks and incandescent lighting. *Courtesy of Port Authority of Allegheny County.*

Washington Tunnel Co. to complete what had become an astoundingly expensive project. The Philadelphia Company, in exchange, received stock in the Mount Washington Tunnel Co. At the same time, newspapers reported that the Pittsburgh Railways Co., a subsidiary of the Philadelphia Company, had purchased for $1.00 a perpetual right-of-way and assumed all financial responsibility for the approaches and tunnel from the Mount Washington Tunnel Company. Pittsburgh Railways president James Callery, vice president S.L. Tone and general superintendent John Murphy all saw the benefit in having the streetcar company control the tunnel and transit lines that would use it and had encouraged the Philadelphia Company's involvement to ensure completion of the tunnel. To that end, it was also reported that in early January 1903, the Philadelphia Company had contracted with Booth and Flinn to build the tunnel. Booth and Flinn later purchased the Pittsburg Tunnel Co. and its rights to the tunnel for $32,000 and reimbursed Nicholson Co. $779.83 for construction costs. Some speculated that the Pittsburg Tunnel Co. never intended to construct a tunnel but used the conflict to its financial advantage.

Passengers exiting Carrick streetcar at the South Hills Junction stop, June 1916. *Courtesy of Archives & Special Collections, University of Pittsburgh Library System.*

TUNNEL DESCRIPTION

Amos D. Neeld, a Crafton, Pennsylvania tunnel and bridge engineer, designed the $2 million Mount Washington Tunnel. Booth and Flinn Ltd. employed three hundred men, working day and night for over two years to "excavate, construct, [and] complete the tunnel…through Mt. Washington in the City of Pittsburgh, as well as furnish all labor, equipment, machinery and material." To expedite construction, two crews working simultaneously from both ends bored through Mount Washington.

The tunnel is 3,492 feet long. Its horseshoe-shaped entryways are 40 feet high and 44 feet wide and are faced with Beaver County sandstone. The tunnel interior measured from the top of the rails to the inside of the center of the arch is $19\frac{1}{2}$ feet high and 24 feet wide at its base. The tunnel's concrete walls are 22 inches thick and extend 1 foot below the level of the excavated tunnel. About 7.5 million bricks line the walls. Strands of incandescent lights traversed the length of the tunnel. Double ninety-pound standard T tracks mounted on white oak ties in a bed of crushed blue stone permitted cars to travel simultaneously north and south. The tracks connected at the north end to a three-track turnout at Sycamore and Carson Streets.

TUNNEL GRADE

The tunnel's elevation decreases 204.54 feet, from 954.90 feet at the South Portal to 750.36 feet at the North Portal. At the south end, the first 100.00 feet of the tunnel are level. The tunnel then slopes downward about 5.86 feet for every 100.00 feet over the rest of its length and results in an overall grade of 5.86 percent. The accompanying graph shows the change in grade from the South to the North Portal.

The tunnel's almost straight design allowed street railway engineers and workers to see through the tunnel from either end. There is a slight curve at about 1,200 feet from the South Portal as the tunnel passes under Tuscola Street in Mount Washington. From the North Portal to Carson Street, the elevation declines another almost 11 to 740 feet, and the tracks curve just beyond the northern exit of the tunnel.

To permit safe travel through the tunnel, Pittsburgh Railways Co. reportedly set a standard car travel time of four minutes from the South Portal at the South Hills Junction to the North Portal at Carson and Smithfield Streets. The optimal speed for a car to meet the standard was 9.92 miles per hour.

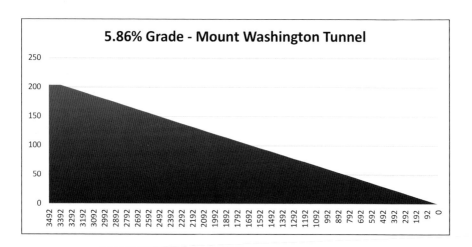

Opposite: Curve in track at the North Portal of the Mount Washington Tunnel at Carson Street. White spot at left inside tunnel is the South Portal. *Photo by author.*

CONSTRUCTION TIMELINE—MOUNT WASHINGTON TUNNEL

Intermittent newspaper accounts described the progress of the Mount Washington Tunnel project.

June 3, 1902: Construction begins on the Mount Washington Tunnel Co. tunnel.

September 26, 1902: Workmen digging the shaft for the Mount Washington Tunnel Co. will go as deep into the hill as is necessary.

October 6, 1902: Ground was broken on north end of tunnel. By the end of October, work also began at the south end. Two shifts of thirty men working day and night, six days per week bored from both directions. Construction progressed at the rate of 300 feet per month or 5.62 feet per day. Pittsburgh's landslide-prone red bed clay (the combination of shale and clay) soil made tunnel building dangerous. Great care was taken to prevent accidents.

April 14, 1903: Two workers killed and two injured in a dynamite explosion inside the tunnel just after the start of the workday. Preparations were completed the prior evening to blast a large quantity of rock on the north end of the tunnel. When the dynamite didn't detonate, the foreman and several workers, thinking the fuse was faulty, approached the dynamite. It unexpectedly exploded and sent workers fleeing the mass of falling rock. When the men reached the tunnel entrance, they realized four men were missing. Some went back into tunnel and found the dead and injured. The foreman, Ladordes Lormoresto, age thirty-five, had suffered the full force of the blast and falling rock. Guesseppe Tenazalia, a machine operator, age thirty, also died in the accident. Both resided at 30 Morris Street, Mount Washington. Two others, one with a broken leg and badly bruised, the other not badly injured, were not identified.

June 5, 1903: The Philadelphia Company takes over Mount Washington Tunnel Co. project and provides funding to compete the tunnel's construction.

June 22, 1903: Dumping cars carrying rock and debris run out of control at the Mount Washington Tunnel Company site. Seven workers were hurt.

October 5, 1903: One year after work began, the Mount Washington Tunnel bore was completed when workers broke through the rock at about 2:00 p.m. A rush of wind passed through the length of the tunnel with such force after the last blast of dynamite that workers on the north end were knocked to the ground. Steam shovels then lowered the tunnel floor by eleven feet. The walls would then be bricked and an arched roof built.

June 2, 1904: The tunnel's stone facing, forty feet high and four feet thick, at the North and South Portals completed.

July 15, 1904: William Flinn visited the construction site in response to reported dissatisfaction among the two hundred laborers and fifty bricklayers working on the tunnel's interior. No further mention of worker unrest occurred. Flinn was reportedly satisfied with tunnel progress.

October 6, 1904: A year from the start of interior construction, the last brick was put in place. A large American flag was raised at the Carson Street entrance by P.E. Hanley, a New York tunnel engineer. Two hundred workers cheered.

November 11, 1904: Workers laid the last track.

TUNNEL OPENS

On November 30, 1904, two cars, one named Pittsburg, from the South Hills Junction, the other from the Carson Street, carrying representatives of the Pittsburgh Railways Co., Beechwood Improvement Co, Hilltop Boards of Trade and local newspapers made inaugural trips through the tunnel. Residents from Mount Washington and Duquesne Heights cheered heartily. Women, in demonstrations of enthusiastic approval, tooted tin horns, clanged bells and thumped on frying pans and coffee pots as the cars rumbled through the tunnel. Seven miles of street

Pittsburgh Railways Co. officials and newspaper reporters were the first to ride through the Mount Washington Tunnel from the South Portal at the South Hills Junction near Warrington Avenue to the North Portal at Carson and Smithfield Streets on November 30, 1904. The first trip for local residents occurred on December 1, 1904, at 5:05 a.m. *Reprint from* Pittsburgh Gazette, *December 1, 1904.*

railways now had rapid access to downtown. The first trip through the Mount Washington tunnel with actual passengers occurred at 5:05 a.m. on December 1, 1904.

In 1919, the Pennsylvania Public Service Commission's Snow Report concluded, stating:

> *The real estate development did not materialize* [after the tunnel was opened] *as rapidly as had been contemplated; but there can be no doubt as to the great benefit which inured to the public generally in the chain of boroughs located on the South Hills and finally connected to the railways operated through the tunnel and over Smithfield St. Bridge into the city, where before the transportation was indirect....After the cars were run through the tunnel a considerable savings of time was affected and the development of the territory in these municipalities was speeded up. The Mt. Washington Tunnel has been indispensable to transportation facilities of Greater Pittsburgh.*

6
THE ST. LOUIS CAR CO. SERIES 4200 CAR

Knoxville #4236 was one of fifty cars placed into service by the Pittsburgh Railways Co. in 1914. The cars built by the St. Louis Car Company are distinguished by their order number, 996, and their series, 4200. Many of the 4200 Series cars remained in use until the mid-1940s.

The Knoxville streetcar line was one of about one hundred formerly independent street railway companies acquired through leases and purchases in the late 1800s and early 1900s by the Pittsburgh Railways Co., a subsidiary of the Philadelphia Company, an organization formed by George Westinghouse. The Philadelphia Company owned all of Pittsburgh Railways Co.'s common and preferred stock and received almost all of the company's dividends, while the Pittsburgh Railways Co. paid all expenses for operations, ordinary maintenance, taxes and interest and rentals of the underlying companies. Data from 1918, a year after the Knoxville trolley accident, indicates the extent of the service provided by the Pittsburgh Railways Co.: 264 million passengers traveled over 33.6 million miles.

The 4200 Series car evolved from one first introduced in 1905. The low-floor steel cars with a vintage appearance were designed by P.N. Jones, a Pittsburgh Railways Co. mechanical and electrical engineer who later served as the company's superintendent and general manager.

The trolley was 45 feet long, 8 feet and 2 inches wide and 10 feet and 4 inches high and had double trucks (wheels) with four motors and four axles. It weighed about eighty-eight thousand pounds and had an internal floor area of 344 square feet, with seating for fifty-five passengers and space for twenty-nine standees. Car #4236 was "double-ended" and designed to operate with a motorman and conductor. It could be driven from either end, which eliminated the need for a loop turnaround track at the end of a route. The car had a single front door and double center doors. Its floor sloped downward between the double trucks and toward the center doors. The lower floor required fewer steps, which made it easier and quicker for passengers to enter and exit and ultimately reduced a car's running time. The fare box and emergency brake stood in the center of the car. The motorman used a seven-notch controller also designed by P.N. Jones to operate the car. A bronze wheel attached to the trolley pole spun about five thousand times each and every mile as it moved along an electrified copper wire.

The Jones low-floor steel side entrance car was described as being equipped with every modern device for the safety of the passengers and represented the most modern and substantial construction of its time. Images from the Pennsylvania Trolley Museum and Washington University in St. Louis detail the car's construction.

The St. Louis Car Company, founded in 1887, built streetcars, rail cars, automobiles and airplanes over its eighty-eight-year history. In the late 1890s,

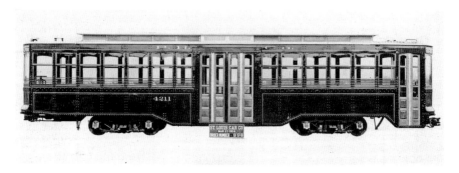

Above: St. Louis Car Co. builder's photo, car #4211, March 1914, Pittsburgh Railways Co. Order 996, 1914. Notice the double trucks (wheels) and raised eaves atop the roof of the car. *Courtesy of Miller Library, Pennsylvania Trolley Museum, Washington, P.A.*

Opposite, top: Construction plans, Pittsburgh Railways Co. #4200 Series Cars. The drawing specifies the use of Westinghouse Airbrakes. The lower left corner details the construction of the six-foot over deck eaves on top of the car. *Courtesy of Miller Library, Pennsylvania Trolley Museum, Washington, P.A.*

Opposite, bottom: Blueprint seating arrangement, Pittsburgh Railways Co. #4200 Series Cars. The car's stated seating capacity was fifty-five. Passengers sat around the perimeter of the car. Note seats at both ends surround the motorman's operating position. The width of the front door is two feet, four and a half inches and the center double doors are five feet wide. *Courtesy of Miller Library, Pennsylvania Trolley Museum, Washington, P.A.*

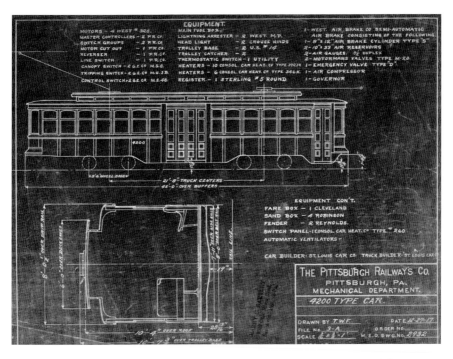

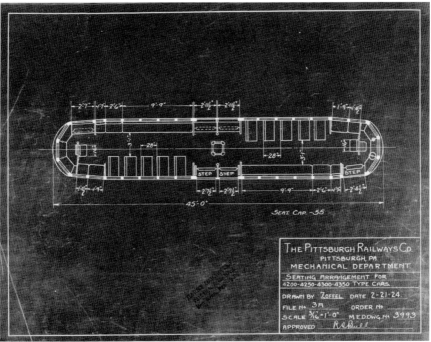

Above: St. Louis Car Co. front view of car #4211, Pittsburgh Railways Co, #4200 Series Cars, Order 996, 1914. *Courtesy of Department of Special Collections, Washington University Libraries, St. Louis, MO.*

Opposite: St. Louis Car Co. photo of Motorman's Cab, Pittsburgh Railways Co. #4200 Series Cars, Order 996, 1914. *Courtesy of Department of Special Collections, Washington University Libraries, St. Louis, MO.*

with the transition from horse drawn to the electrification of street railway systems and as one of the top three street railway car building companies, it benefited from a growing national and international demand for trolleys. The St. Louis region's sizable skilled German immigrant population provided a ready workforce for the company's foundry and woodworking facilities. About 75 percent of the car components were produced in the company's wood, steel and iron shops, while car wheels, electrical equipment, plate glass,

Left: St. Louis Car Co. photo of interior of #4200 Series Cars, Pittsburgh Railways Co. Order 996, 1914. *Courtesy of Department of Special Collections, Washington University Libraries, St. Louis, MO.*

Below: Fare box and conductor's emergency brake in the middle of the car near center double doors, Pittsburgh Railways Co. #4200 Series Cars. *Courtesy of Miller Library, Pennsylvania Trolley Museum, Washington, PA.*

St. Louis Car Co. photo of car's steel body and roof deck frames, Pittsburgh Railways Co. #4200 Series Cars, Order 996, 1914. The framework for the deck roof is visible in this photo. *Courtesy of Department of Special Collections, Washington University Libraries, St. Louis, MO.*

paint and canvas were subcontracted. About 250 employees manufactured about four hundred streetcars per year.

In the early 1900s, the St. Louis Car Co. was one of the first manufacturers to use steel rather than wood in cars to increase their structural integrity. From its founding until the mid-1930s, the St. Louis Car Co. had no standard car design. Instead, it relied on collaboration between the buyers and St. Louis Car Co. engineers to produce designs to meet buyer preferences. Buyers could specify trucks, motors and the controller system, in addition to fittings, trim, hardware, sash, flooring, heating, couplers, signage, lighting fixtures, batteries, seats, and door actuators.

The earliest horse-drawn streetcars tended to be ornate with a single truck and an open or closed design. The time from 1896 through the mid-1930s was marked by a transition to elongated, spacious cars with double trucks to provide greater passenger capacity and maximize owner profits. Passenger comfort was generally absent from design consideration. Those who relied

St. Louis Car Co. photo of car's wood outer body construction and deck roof, Pittsburgh Railways Co. #4200 Series Cars, Order 996, 1914. The deck roof is clearly visible in this photo. *Courtesy of Department of Special Collections, Washington University Libraries, St. Louis, MO.*

on street railways for transportation endured crowded, uncomfortable and badly ventilated cars and either froze or suffocated from season to season.

The Pittsburgh Railways Co. was a long and loyal St. Louis Car Co. customer. Through cooperation with St. Louis Car Co. prior to 1914, Pittsburgh Railways Co. created its own standard steel, low-floor, Jones-type, or "Pittsburgh," car with its signature deck roof and center double doors. From the early 1900s to 1936, Pittsburgh Railways Co. bought about 650 of the Pittsburgh cars. The St. Louis Car Co. and Pittsburgh Railways Co. both believed the deck roof provided excellent ventilation, even though it caused structural weakness in the car body. In St. Louis Car Co.'s Catalog No. 105, published in 1927, of the twenty most important cars in the company's product line, only the Pittsburgh car had a raised deck roof. The Pittsburgh car persisted until the mid-1930s, when the introduction of the President's Conference Car, which eliminated the deck roof, rendered the Pittsburgh car obsolete.

PART III.

THE AFTERMATH

7

ACCIDENT INVESTIGATION AND CORONER'S INQUEST

Coroner's Inquest, a public proceeding initiated and conducted by the county coroner that relies on witness testimony to determine the cause and manner of death in instances when the death is sudden, unexpected or disaster-related. A jury generally of 6 local residents may be called to assist with the inquest. If a jury determines that an accidental death is blameworthy, criminal prosecution may follow.

Pittsburgh police officers stationed at the intersection of Carson and Smithfield Streets immediately notified the Allegheny County Coroner's Office of the accident. Pittsburgh mayor Joseph G. Armstrong, public safety director Charles S. Hubbard, police superintendent W. Noble Matthews and coroner Samuel C. Jamison and his deputies responded within minutes. Jamison took charge of the accident scene, and with the help of his chief deputy, George Ambos, initiated an investigation while other deputies worked to recover and transport victims to the morgue on Diamond Street. Jamison and Ambos went to South Side Hospital to interview the motorman, but they found he was still unconscious.

Jamison's first public comments focused on reassuring the victims, their families and the public. He also disclosed that his deputies had already verified where Klingler had been in the hours after leaving home on Mount Washington and before he reported to the South Hills tunnel barn for duty at 3:00 p.m.

Early on December 25, the coroner and his deputies, George Ambos and H.T. Ewing; John Dohoney; Pittsburgh Railways physician, Wilber Holtz; and Pittsburgh Railways general manager, P.N. Jones, interviewed the motorman and conductor at South Side Hospital. Reportedly, Klingler exhibited no emotion when responding to questions, which caused the coroner to think that the motorman might not be of sound mind. His description fundamentally differed from the statement he gave to Deputy Coroner George Ambos on Christmas Eve and those of other witnesses. According to Klingler, "I took charge of car at the south end of the tunnel, it being my first trip for the day. When my car got about 500 feet into tunnel, I noticed that it was gaining momentum and I applied my airbrake. The brake refused to work and it seemed that there was no brake there at all. I quickly applied my handbrake, but the car had gained such speed by this time that the brakes would not hold. I then applied my reverse, but it did not hold because my overhead switch went off."

Jamison asked if the car stopped when the trolley came off the wire. The motorman responded, "No, sir. The car never stopped until it crashed into the pole at the end of the tunnel." Jamison then said, "We have information that your trolley pole left the wire and that you had an argument with your conductor as to who should adjust the trolley pole." Klingler replied, "I have no knowledge of the trolley coming off after we left the south end of the tunnel." Dohoney then asked, "When you were attempting to apply your brakes, were you interfered with by the passengers?" Klinger answered, "The passengers did crowd up around the front door, but they did not bother me; they had left their seats in preparation for getting off the car at Carson St. I stuck to my post until the crash came and from that time on, I did not remember anything more until I regained consciousness in the hospital."

When questioned by the coroner, Klingler vigorously denied that he had consumed intoxicating liquor before going on duty but admitted that he had been drinking at a club on Second Avenue at 1:00 a.m. the morning of the disaster. He also denied being at Fuhs Saloon in the afternoon prior to the wreck.

On December 26, the coroner charged Klingler with manslaughter, and the deputies placed him under arrest. The coroner's office instructed the hospital to keep Klingler in a private room and barred visitors except for family members and law enforcement officials. Jamison also ordered the clerks in his office to not issue bond for Klingler's release. Pittsburgh police guarded the door to Klingler's hospital room around the clock.

The group then proceeded to the Mount Washington car barns, where they were joined by Pittsburgh Railways president S.L. Tone for interviews with Martin Joyce and LeRoy Hazelbacker.

Knoxville #4236 conductor Martin Joyce told the investigators:

> *We were to leave at 3:03 o'clock, but the crew that we relieved was 6 minutes late. As soon as the car got underway, I immediately began taking the report of the register, and did not pay any attention to the operator of the car. When we got a short distance, the trolley came off, and, not being able to leave the car, I asked the motorman to adjust the trolley pole. The trolley was put on the wire by someone, I don't know who, and we started through the tunnel. I resumed taking the report of the register, and in a few seconds, I noticed that the car was going too rapid, and I looked up in the direction of the motorman who was working the brakes. I then realized the car was running away. When the crash came, I was thrown under the fare box and it saved me from being killed. The crowd was kept from smothering me by the box, which shielded me.*

Jamison asked, "Did you have an argument with the motorman as to who should put the trolley on?" Joyce responded, "When I saw that I could not leave the car I asked the motorman to put it on, but he did not leave his cab." Jamison then asked, "Did the motorman reply that he would not put it on, and that that was your work?" Joyce replied, "I did not hear him say anything after I asked him to put the trolley on."

The group then talked with Charleroi Car motorman Leroy Hazelbaker, who said:

> *My car was but a few hundred feet in the tunnel when my headlights showed that another car had stopped a few feet in front of me. The lights of the car were out, but I was able to see that it was very crowded. Looking up I saw that the trolley was off the car and knowing that the conductor could not get out to adjust the trolley pole, I left my cab and put the trolley on the wire. I then gave a signal for the motorman to go ahead. At first the stalled car remaining stationary for a few seconds, and then all at once the motorman seemed to start off quite rapidly.*

After Hazelbaker was told that Klingler said the car did not stop, he replied, "The car did stop and I put on the trolley, because I thought I was doing my duty."

The group then traveled through the Mount Washington Tunnel on a special trolley from the South Hills Junction in an attempt to ascertain why the brakes on the Knoxville car failed to operate. As Jamison and Dohoney rode beside the operator of the car, Eugene C. Fitch, Pittsburgh Railways' superintendent of tunnel barns, explained that there were four sets of brakes—air, hand, dynamic and power. Fitch affirmed that either the dynamic or air brake should have stopped the car. He demonstrated that if Klingler had used either the dynamic or air brakes, he could have brought his car to a stop, even if the overhead switches had gone off.

The last stop was the West Park barns in McKees Rocks to inspect the wrecked car. There, the men saw that one brake rod was broken on the car's rear trucks and were advised that the rod had to have broken under stress caused when the car left the rails at the North Portal of the tunnel because it could not have happened while the car was still running on the rails in the tunnel.

On December 26, Coroner Jamison, when speaking to reporters later in the day, said that "the matter is now well in hand and we will have no trouble in positively placing the blame where it belongs when the inquest is conducted." He predicted that "there would be 'nothing startling' in the revelations to be made at the inquest."

Overall, evidence suggested that the cause of tragedy was not the breakdown of machinery but the human element that fails in vital moments. Other motormen believed that Klingler simply lost his head and failed to use emergency measures that might have prevented the catastrophe.

The Pittsburgh Railways Co. also conducted a separate accident investigation. On December 26 and 27, the company's president, S.L. Tone; general manager, P.N. Jones; superintendent, James Loftis; and equipment superintendent, F.R. Phillips, met with conductors, motormen and other witnesses at the Philadelphia Company Building. Their intent was not only to identify the cause of the accident but also to meet regulatory requirements. The company, by law, had to submit a report to the Pennsylvania Public Service Commission when any accident resulted in physical injury. Based on the report, the commission could issue orders mandating the length of experience and the general abilities of employees who operate the company's cars. The scope and outcomes of the company's inquiry are unknown.

Coroner Jamison announced on December 27 that the motorman was under arrest and that available evidence suggested that he was partially intoxicated when he took over the Knoxville trolley at the tunnel entrance.

On December 29, Klingler was released from South Side Hospital. Before transporting the motorman to the county jail, Chief Deputy Coroner George Ambos and Deputy Coroner Harry Ewing took him to the Coroner's Office for further interrogation. At that time, Jamison asked, "What did you do so far as you can remember the day preceding the accident and until the time of the accident?"

Klingler, staring blankly, responded,

> *Sunday I went to my brother's home in Carrick and helped him trim a Christmas tree. Later I went to a club in Second Avenue in the city and went home about 1 o'clock Monday morning. I got up about 5 o'clock and reporting for duty, took my car and worked until about 9 o'clock. Then I went home and later to my brother's, where I remained until 2:15 when I went to the barns and waited until time to take out my car. I took out the car about 3:15 and it got away from me in the tunnel. The brakes wouldn't work and then the crash came.*

Jamison then asked, "Had you taken a drink during Sunday at the club or Monday prior to going to work?" Klingler replied, "I had taken some liquor at the club at intervals." Then asked if he was in Fuhs Saloon in Mount Washington, Klingler said he did not remember being there nor did he remember being in a butcher shop on Boggs Avenue.

Jamison said, "You seem to be mistaken about your story…and I am going to send you to jail now. I want you to think over the events leading up to this accident, where you were on Sunday and what you drank. When you feel that you have remembered all that happened during that time, send for me." Jamison then ordered Klingler be taken to jail and asked the county physician to assess Klingler's sanity. Jail guards were told to keep a close watch on him while he is in their custody.

Late on December 26, Klingler sent Jamison a letter stating that he wanted a chance to tell his story and that his mind went blank when he was previously asked about the trolley going off the wire. Klingler confirmed that the trolley came off the wire and the car stopped but was also steadfast in saying that he did not run the car through the tunnel in a reckless manner and refuted the coroner's accusation that he was intoxicated.

DISTRICT ATTORNEY ACTS

As deaths mounted and funerals took place in the days following the accident, tensions surrounding the investigation grew. District Attorney R.H. Jackson also undertook a full investigation. He declined to call for a special grand jury, deferring to one that was already scheduled to meet on January 7, 1918. Jackson concluded from his "investigation of the disaster, the motorman was not drunk." Instead, the investigation turned to the operation of the streetcar and consideration of whether "the brakes refused to work or that the motorman becoming excited, failed to use all the means at his disposal to stop the car." He stated that he had enough evidence against the motorman to support a prima facie case of manslaughter but would not proceed with a grand jury investigation unless the coroner's jury chose not to recommend Klingler for trial. Jackson left the decision regarding the negligence of the Pittsburgh Railways Co. officials to the coroner.

The coroner's investigation lasted less than a week. By December 29, Jamison determined that an inquest to fix responsibility for the tunnel accident would be held as soon as victims were released from local hospitals and able to participate. He commented, "So far as I can see now, a motorman who lost his head and who had been drinking is responsible for this terrible calamity," and added, "The [Pittsburgh Railways] officials, as I can see it, are not criminally responsible." In closing, he said, "It must be understood that the inquest has nothing to do with streetcar situation, which I also agree is abominable. We are trying to decide who is responsible for this horrible accident." In response to Jamison's request for a special legal counsel to represent the Commonwealth's interests, the Allegheny County Commissioners appointed Richard W. Martin.

Martin later stated that to hold Pittsburgh Railways responsible, "it would have to be alleged that the company knew of the motorman's bad habits and still permitted him to work."

A jury of six reputable businessmen would examine the facts and decide whether a recommendation to the grand jury or any other kind of criticism or recommendation should be made concerning the Pittsburgh Railways Co. officials or employees.

The question of whether the motorman was intoxicated when the accident occurred remained unresolved. Jamison believed evidence of intoxication existed, although Jackson did not. The issue loomed over the proceedings that followed.

DOHONEY CONCLUDES CARELESSNESS AND OVERCROWDING

The Public Service Commission's head investigator, John P. Dohoney, was responsible for determining whether the tunnel wreck was due to a mechanical malfunction of the car or human error. Dohoney filed his report with Harrisburg on Wednesday, December 26, after completing an inspection of the tunnel and wrecked car. The next day, the commission requested additional information from the Pittsburgh Railways Co., including a comprehensive map of the tunnel, its southern approaches, the curve at the Northern Portal and details related to the accident scene at Smithfield and Carson Streets for use in the development of recommendations to prevent future accidents. The commission's formal report was released on January 16, 1918, prior to the Public Service Commission's hearing in Pittsburgh.

Dohoney concluded that the Knoxville car's safety equipment was in good condition when the car entered the Mount Washington Tunnel and implied that the motorman's carelessness and overcrowding caused the accident. He found the air brakes were in effective working condition to operate the car at the speed necessary to travel through the tunnel in four minutes and said that it was evident that the car was stopped by the brakes when the trolley went off the wire after it entered the tunnel. Dohoney stated that the condition of the brakes is critical because it appears "that the memory of the motorman was faulty as to some of the circumstances attending the disaster." An inspection of the brakes after the accident indicated that they were not damaged sufficiently to prevent control of the car by the motorman, and he believed that after the trolley was placed back on the wire, the motorman allowed the car to "attain a degree of speed that precluded his efforts to bring it under control before it reached the point of derailment." In fact, the car's speed was so excessive that the car left the tracks when it reached the slight curve in the tracks at the north end of the tunnel, turned over on its side and slid two hundred feet, colliding with a steel pole. The collision shattered the car and killed and injured many passengers.

Dohoney made several recommendations. The Pittsburgh Railways Co. should institute procedures to mitigate overcrowding and permit all safety equipment (brakes) to be operated by the motorman or conductor without hindrance. Where there are curves at the bottom of grades, the height of the outer rail (track) should be increased to help prevent derailments. In addition, because of the substantial grades the trolleys must traverse in the region, the company should ensure that cars are maintained and operated

The Allegheny County morgue, Diamond Street. *Courtesy of Archives & Special Collections, University of Pittsburgh Library System.*

with extreme caution. "The brakes should be thoroughly and frequently tested and the speed so regulated that the cars will never get beyond the control of the motorman. The enforcement of regulations in this direction is absolutely essential if the passengers are to be safeguarded in the manner to which they are entitled."

Coroner's Inquest

The coroner's inquest convened on February 20, 1918. Well before the inquest began, the hearing room at the coroner's office on Diamond Street was crowded to capacity with friends and family members of those killed or injured, Knoxville Borough and civic organization representatives and Pittsburgh Railways Co. officials and employees. Coroner Samuel Jamison presided. Allegheny County solicitor Richard W. Martin represented the commonwealth. William J. Brennen represented H.H. Klingler, and William D. Challener acted on behalf of the Pittsburgh Railways Co. William D. Grimes, attorney for Knoxville Borough, and Frank I. Gosser were also present at the counsel table.

Six local businessmen sat as coroner's jurors: Eli Edmundson Jr., age sixty-six, stockbroker, 255 Meyran Avenue, Oakland; F.J. Bergold, age thirty-six, insurance broker, 1002 Bidwell Street, North Side; Jesse C. Davis, age forty-six, Alderman Fourteenth Ward/fire insurance agent, 5708 Darlington Road, Squirrel Hill; Clarence L. Saxton, age thirty-nine, real estate broker, William Penn Hotel, downtown; Michael J. McMahon, age fifty-four, printer, 2 Stowe Street, Ingram; and Harry Beegle, age forty-four, auto supply merchant, 5817 Phillips Avenue, Squirrel Hill.

The inquest started promptly at 10:00 a.m. Deputy Coroner George Ambos brought Herman H. Klingler into the room. Klingler was described as looking quite tired and nervous. Jamison called Klingler as the first witness and explained that he was not required to testify, but any testimony he gave could be used against him in court. The inquest was delayed until Klingler's attorney, William J. Brennen, arrived. Brennen recommended that Klingler not be the first to testify, but could at some point if other testimony made it necessary.

Twenty witnesses, including Pittsburgh Railways employees, accident victims and local businesspeople, were called. The clerk's handwritten record of their testimony mirrored the news reports immediately following the accident and reflected a consistency of arguments that carried through to the trial. The following verbatim testimony from reporters at the inquest for *some* of the witnesses provides a sense of the inquiry. Jamison and Martin questioned the witnesses.

Martin Joyce, age twenty-two, was the conductor on Knoxville #4236 and the first to testify. A *Pittsburgh Sun* reporter recorded Jamison and Joyce's dialog. Joyce started by stating: "I took the car at the south end of the tunnel. It was overcrowded, probably 118 passengers on the car. In fact, there were as many passengers as could get on. When the car proceeded into the tunnel about three or four lengths the trolley jumped off, and then the car stopped."

Jamison asked, "Who put the trolley on?"

Joyce responded, "Motorman Leroy Hazelbacker of the Charleroi line."

Jamison: "Did you see where the motorman was?"

Joyce: "No."

Jamison: "When did you notice that the car was getting beyond the control of the motorman?"

Joyce: "When it was about half way through the tunnel."

Jamison: "Could you use your brake?"

Joyce: "No, the car was so crowded with passengers that it was impossible."

Jamison: "Why did you let the car get overcrowded?"

Joyce: "These passengers were permitted to get on the car by the other crew which we relieved at the tunnel."

Jamison: "Does the company issue instructions to the employees as to the overcrowding of street cars?"

Joyce: "No. We have no limit to the number of passengers that may board our cars."

Jamison: "Whom did you report to before you went on duty?"

Joyce: "Dispatcher Maley."

Attorney Richard W. Martin then asked the witness: "Have you any idea how fast the car was going?"

Joyce: "I would judge the car was going as fast as it goes down grade… about 50 miles per hour"

Michael Francis Maley, age forty-seven, was the day dispatcher at south end of the tunnel who assigned the crew to Knoxville #4236 on the day of the accident.

Jamison asked, "What is your method of choosing crews?"

Maley responded, "We generally select them the day before. Klingler appeared at the barn at 10:00 a.m., December 24, and I him told to report at 3:01 p.m. for duty." Maley noted that "Arlington" was Klingler's regular run.

Jamison: "What was his condition?"

Maley: "All right. He walked into the room at 2:54 p.m. and called 'All right, Mike,' and I checked him off." Maley then explained that he could only look through a small window from his perch and said the car came in loaded from Knoxville. The other crew had left the car. Conductor Joyce was assigned the day before.

Martin asked, "Had Klingler worked the day before?"

Maley: "No. He did not show up. He had not worked for several days." Maley also stated that Klingler had worked for the company about six or seven months prior to the accident.

Jamison: "Have you any rules regarding motormen and conductors drinking intoxicating liquors?"

Maley: "Yes a man who uses intoxicating liquor is not allowed to work."

Joseph Mary, age sixty, was a night dispatcher at south end of the tunnel who saw Klingler on day of accident.

Jamison asked, "Do you know Mr. Klingler?"

Mary responded, "Yes.…He came to the barn at 4:25 a.m., December 24 and said he had been off for several days as a result of illness and that he was ready to go to work."

Mary stated that he put Klingler on the board and that Klingler had given him a chain and ten-dollar gold piece to keep for him. The motorman did not show any signs of liquor, and the dispatcher permitted him to take the 6-01 red car out for three trips.

Jamison: "What was his condition?"

Mary: "Apparently, normal."

Edward Froube, age thirty-four: Motorman Froube testified that Klingler, someone he had known for six to seven months, got on his car about 2:00 a.m. at the south end of the tunnel and rode to Prospect Street on December 24. He said Klingler was in his usual condition, "talkative," but could not say whether Klingler had been drinking and did not smell liquor. He also reported that there was nothing unusual about Klingler.

Peter Spiker (**Speicher**), age thirty-two: Motorman Spiker stated that he did not have any conversation with Motorman Froube on day of accident about Klinger being drunk.

John Stadelman, age sixty: A butcher who worked at George Klingler's butcher shop on Brownsville Road, Carrick. Stadelman saw Klingler about noon on the day of the accident. He said Klingler looked to be in good condition and that he did not see Klingler drink anything. Stadelman saw empty bottles in the back room about 10:00 a.m.

Alois W. Winter, age thirty-three: Grocer located next door to George Klingler's butcher shop. Winter saw Klingler in the butcher shop on day of the accident for two or three minutes and said he appeared to be all right before dinner. Winter went into a back room for a drink, where there was a quart bottle of liquor and two cases of beer.

August T. Fuhs, age forty: Hotel proprietor. Klingler was in his hotel on Southern Avenue about 2:00 p.m. on Christmas Eve.

Henry Allews, age fifty: Bartender at Fuhs Hotel. Allews refused to serve Klingler at about 2:30 p.m. on December 24. Allews testified that Klingler had asked for whiskey and he refused him, as "he was in uniform, looked sleepy, he may have been drinking, could not say. He did not look good to me."

John D. Schimmel, age fifty: A local butcher who saw Klingler about 3:00 p.m. on December 24. Klingler was under the influence of liquor. Schimel said he talked to Klingler. Klingler was six or seven blocks from the South Hills car barn.

Charles A. Freeborn, age forty-four: City detective. Freeborn boarded the Knoxville car at Orchard Street. He stated that the car ran to the tunnel, where there was a change in crew. The car then started and ran into the tunnel three or four car lengths. The trolley came off the car, and the car stopped. Conductor Joyce hollered several times at Motorman Klingler to put the trolley back on the wire. When the trolley lights came on, the car started rapidly. The conductor could not operate the emergency brake in the center of the car. He did not have room to get to it. Freeborn was standing near the fare box and said 114 car fares were rung up. He could not see the motorman.

George B. McBee, age fourteen: McBee was in the rear of the car. He said when the trolley came off in the tunnel, the motorman from the Charleroi car put the trolley on, and the car then started off.

H.B. Carroll, age thirty-two: P&LE Railroad engineer. Carroll got on the car in Knoxville. He said the car was full. The motorman got on the car. Carroll observed nothing unusual. He said:

> *I walked up front towards the Motorman...stood next to the motorman... as the car filled up. When we got into tunnel, the trolley jumped off. The Conductor hollered at Motorman to put on the trolley, and he said it was not his duty. After hearing the bell to proceed, at about 3:15 p.m., Klingler threw on controller, the car was going 50–60 miles per hour. He did not throw the controller off until the car reached a point about 500 feet from the north end of the tunnel. He then applied the airbrakes. He applied it lightly at first and then full. The speed of the car was reduced to about 30–35 miles per hour and was traveling at that speed when it overturned. Klingler didn't apply any other brake. Car was going 30–35 miles per hour when it struck the curve in the track at Carson Street.*

Leroy Hazelbaker, age thirty-five: Motorman at Castle Shannon Division. On December 24, as Hazelbaker's car was drifting into tunnel, he saw a car laying in the dark inside the tunnel. He put his brakes on safely, got off his car and put the trolley on. He hollered to the crew, and the Knoxville car started off at the usual rate of speed. It was about 3:15 p.m., and the car was crowded. He did not see the car upset, as four minutes must be consumed from South Portal of the tunnel to Carson Street.

A.P. Schenk, age thirty-five: Motorman who turned Knoxville #4236 over to Klingler at the south end of the tunnel. He stated that he had made four trips, and the brakes were in order. There was nothing wrong when he left the car. He saw Klingler after the car turned over but observed nothing unusual about him.

Thomas Connelly: Night foreman at South Hills car barns. He stated that it was his duty to make sure the car was inspected and confirmed that Jacob Bajaczyk/Bajaiyk, age forty-seven, 58 (rear) Twenty-Second Street, South Side, and John Giavanbattista Lombardi, age twenty-six, 165 Southern Avenue, Mount Washington, inspected the car that day.

Frank Reith Phillips, age forty-one: As Pittsburgh Railways' superintendent of equipment, Phillips examined the Knoxville car shortly after the accident and found the car's mechanisms in good condition.

Although he found the pull rod broken and the car lying on its side, he thought the car's trucks would still operate. He confirmed that on impact, the car broke an iron pole and fence and believed that the condition of the air brake showed it had been applied with great force. He noted there were four brakes that could be used to stop the car. In answer to William Brennen's question, "Could this car traveling at 50 miles an hour be brought to a stop in 500 feet?" Phillips answered, "The car could not be stopped in that distance traveling at that speed."

Albert J. Hoffman, age thirty-seven: Driver for Hilltop Ice Co. Hoffman indicated that Klingler came into the Hotel Brandt by himself at 1:00 p.m. and appeared to be under the influence of liquor. Klingler was served by the bartender. Hoffman saw the motorman drink whiskey and a beer.

Harry Poke, age thirty-three: Poke, an employee at Fuhs Bar Room, was present when Henry Allews refused Klingler a drink, although he would not say Klingler was drunk.

John H. Gust, age thirty-three: Gust was in Fuhs Saloon when Klingler refused a drink. He said Klingler appeared to be intoxicated.

George Ambos, age fifty: Allegheny County chief deputy coroner. Ambos testified that Klingler admitted that he had been drinking before the accident. Klingler's attorney objected to the statement.

JAMISON'S CHARGE TO THE JURY

TUNNEL WRECK BLAME FIXED BY CORONER'S JURY

Motorman Is Held for Grand Jury—Dispatcher Arrested as Accessory.

WARNS ON OVERLOADING

Reprint from Pittsburgh Post, *February 21, 1918.*

The coroner in his instructions to the jury stated that "if they believed the motorman of the car was under the influence of liquor, they should bring a verdict charging contribution negligence against the dispatcher who allowed Klingler to take out the car, and a similar verdict should be returned against the conductor of the car if the jury believe that he permitted the car to be overcrowded." Further, Jamison said that if Klingler was believed to be intoxicated, he would be subject to imprisonment and a fine. Four of the witnesses testified that Klingler was intoxicated, and the majority said that he was not. The motorman did not testify. Jury deliberations began at 12:45 p.m.

CORONER'S JURY VERDICT

The jury rendered a verdict after an hour of deliberation. H.H. Klingler was charged with twenty-four counts of manslaughter. Michael F. Maley was charged as an accessory to manslaughter. Martin Joyce was not held because the car was already overcrowded when he took charge of it, and the overcrowding made it impossible for him to reach the emergency brake.

The jury's verdict read:

> [Clara Tanney] *and others came to their death from injuries sustained when Knoxville Street Car # [4236] got beyond control in the tunnel, and running away for a distance of more than 2,000 feet overturned at Smithfield and Carson streets. That Herman H. Klingler, the motorman was grossly careless in the operation of the car. We recommend that Herman H. Klingler be held to await the action of the grand jury in a charge of manslaughter and that M.F. Maley, dispatcher, be held as an accessory to the same.*
>
> *We further recommend that the Pittsburgh Railways Company be more careful in the selection of their employees and that greater scrutiny be made by the Dispatcher before permitting Motormen and Conductors to take charge of cars; we further recommend that the employees be called together to be instructed frequently to their duties for the careful and safe carrying of passengers. The overloading of cars should be prevented and if necessary certain laws should be enacted so that cars would not be loaded beyond their safe operation. It is also recommended that all brake handles shall be kept clear so that they can safely operate. And that the Conductor in charge of the car be held responsible for the safety of passengers.*

Following the verdict, H.H. Klingler was returned to the county jail, and Michael Maley was taken into custody at the Philadelphia Company offices on Grant Street by Deputy Coroner Thomas O'Brien. Maley was later released when the Philadelphia Company secured his bond. The Pittsburgh Railways Co. was not deemed criminally responsible for the accident.

8

CRIMINAL PROSECUTION OF MOTORMAN AND DISPATCHER

Criminal proceedings extended from March 1918 through September 1920. While there are no formal transcripts of the proceedings, news article summaries and newspaper reporters who took verbatim notes provide an understanding of what transpired.

GRAND JURY INDICTS MOTORMAN AND DISPATCHER

The Grand Jury met in Pittsburgh on March 13, 1918, and returned indictments for each death resulting from the Knoxville #4236 car's "wild dash" through the Mount Washington Tunnel on December 24, 1917. Mirroring the recommendations from the coroner's inquest, jury foreman Henry J.V. Wettach reported indictments of involuntary manslaughter against Motorman Herman H. Klingler. The grand jury also believed sufficient evidence existed to indict Michael F. Maley as an accessory before the fact. Twenty-three indictments were handed down against each man.

District Attorney Harry H. Rowand called thirteen witnesses to testify before the grand jury, including Coroner Samuel C. Jamison. All had previously testified at the coroner's inquest. The rest were Martin Joyce, Charles A. Freeborn, Alois W. Winter, Henry Allews, John H. Gust, John D. Schimmel, George B. McBee, H.B. Carroll, Leroy Hazelbacker, A.P. Shenk, Albert J. Hoffman and Harry Poke.

The grand jury also adopted the findings of the coroner's jury regarding streetcar operations. Those recommendations specified that the Pittsburgh Railways Co. should exercise more care in its selection of employees, require greater scrutiny by dispatchers of motormen and conductors before crews are permitted to take charge of cars and provide more frequent instruction of employees on their responsibilities for passenger safety. The jury also recommended that laws should be enacted to prevent overloading of cars, to require that brake handles inside the cars be clear of passengers at all times and to clarify that conductors should be responsible for passenger safety.

Motorman's Trial—February 1919

The trial to determine whether H.H. Klingler and Michael F. Maley were criminally responsible for the deaths of twenty-three people and injuries to eighty-two passengers began on February 10, 1919.

Shortly after the trial convened, attorney James F. Burke, representing Michael F. Maley, petitioned the court to separate Maley's trial from the motorman. Presiding Judge Marshall Brown granted the request. Judge Joseph M. Swearingen was also on the bench for this motion.

Assistant District Attorney Harry Estep then stated that three of twenty-three indictments were chosen for prosecution and Klingler would be tried for involuntary manslaughter in the deaths of Ella C. Sheridan, Gladys C. Sheridan and Clara Tanney. The remaining twenty indictments would be held for prosecution at a later date. The maximum penalty for each indictment, if convicted, was two years. William J. Brennen, Klingler's attorney, objected to the state's decision to try him on only three indictments but was overruled by Judge Joseph M. Swearingen.

Allegheny County coroner's reports described the victims: **Ella C. Sheridan**, age forty-nine, of 218 Brownsville Road, Mount Oliver, died on December 24, 1917, in Mercy Hospital of shock and concussion, severe lacerations of the face and scalp and a compound fracture of the upper jaw; **Clara Tanney**, age thirty-two, 209 Jucunda Street, Knoxville, died on December 24, 1917, at the scene of the accident when her entire body was crushed; and **Gladys H. Sheridan**, age sixteen, daughter of Ella C. Sheridan, died on January 27, 1918, in St. Joseph's Hospital of extensive and severe lacerations to her arms and scalp injuries, blood clots and secondary septicemia due to injuries received in the streetcar wreck.

The trial then proceeded with jury selection and initial testimony. District Attorney Harry Rowand, detective Peter J. McGinty and Sylvester J. Snee, Knoxville Borough solicitor, joined Estep at the prosecutor's table. Klingler, out on bond since the grand jury indicted him, entered the court room with attorney Brennen and several friends just before the trial began. He sat at the rear of the courtroom among passengers and family members of those who were on the "death car." When it was time for the jury selection, he took a seat at the counsel table. It was noted by the press that Brennen was a well-known labor union advocate.

Over sixty prospective jurors were examined. Most had already formed opinions about the case. Among the questions posed to prospective jurors were, "Do you remember the accident at the South Side tunnel on December 24, 1917? Did you read some of the newspaper accounts? Have you formed an opinion or expressed any opinion as to the guilt of the motorman? Did you visit the scene of the accident soon after the wreck? Have you been through the tunnel? Are you in any way related to any person killed or injured in the accident?" In response to some challenges lodged by Brennen, Judge Brown would ask whether an individual could render a verdict based solely on the evidence and the law, regardless of their present opinions. If the answer was yes, Brennen's challenge was overruled.

Twelve men from across the county were ultimately chosen as jurors: Albert Edge, a laborer from Wilkins Township, was the jury foreman; George W. Wilson, a retiree from the Seventh Ward of Pittsburgh; T.D. Harvey, a farmer from Plum Township; James Wheeler Sr., a retiree from the Eighteenth Ward, Pittsburgh; Joseph A. Walter, a clerk from the Twenty-Fourth Ward, Pittsburgh; Charles Young, a retiree from the Ninth Ward, Pittsburgh; Wilbur Soergel, a clerk from West View Borough; Charles T. Manning, a retiree from the Eighth Ward, Pittsburgh; John Hohman, a laborer from the Twenty-Sixth Ward, Pittsburgh; Foster S. Gourley, a clerk from Braddock; Robert Owens, a farmer from Ohio Township; and William A. Dawson, a retiree from the Seventh Ward, Pittsburgh.

In his opening statement to the jury, Assistant District Attorney Estep vowed to prove "that Klingler was under the influence of liquor and that he was operating the car without caution, recklessly and without regard for the safety of the passengers," and given those circumstances, he was going to ask the jury to find him guilty on three charges of involuntary manslaughter.

Of the three witnesses who testified on the first day—Michael Sheridan, who had lost his wife, Ella, and daughter Gladys in the accident; Michael Joyce, the Knoxville #4236 conductor; and Frank W. McGeary, a passenger—Joyce's testimony was the most surprising and potentially damaging to the commonwealth's case. Joyce said he had not seen the motorman before he got on the car and could not comment on Klingler's condition. He said that shortly after the car entered the tunnel, the trolley flew off the wire, but he was unable to leave the crowded car to put the trolley back on. The trolley car sat in the tunnel for about two minutes before the motorman of another car reattached the trolley and the car restarted. Joyce said the car was running fast, but he refused to estimate its speed as it left the tracks at the tunnel's exit. Joyce had changed testimony. At the coroner's inquest, he said the trolley was traveling about fifty miles per hour. He also stated that there was an emergency brake in the middle of the car, but he was unable to reach it because of overcrowding. Although before the accident cars tended to run fast through the tunnel, Joyce confirmed that the running time through the tunnel since the accident had been fixed at four minutes

Frank W. McGeary, a postal employee, boarded the car in Beltzhoover. McGeary said that prior to the accident, as the car traveled down steep Beltzhoover Avenue, it stopped at every corner and the brakes worked. The trolley came off when the car was about twenty-five yards into tunnel and traveled another one hundred yards before it stopped. After several minutes, someone put the trolley back on the wire. After the car started, it began going fast and gained speed until the accident occurred. He realized when the car was about halfway through the tunnel, it was running away. The car swayed from one side to the other, and he did not feel the brakes being applied. He added that before the accident, cars ran through the tunnel at a high rate of speed, but now the cars observe the four-minute rule.

On the second and third days of the trial, fifteen witnesses appeared. Some, including **George McBee**, **Joseph Mary**, **Harry Poke**, **John Gust**, **Alois W. Winter** and **Henry Allews**, recounted testimony they gave at the coroner's inquest and before the grand jury. Others provided new or more detailed evidence. Throughout the day, Klingler sat at the defense table with his head downcast, avoiding eye contact with those who testified.

Dr. George Hays, a physician at Mercy Hospital, said Ella Sheridan was brought to the hospital semiconscious and in very serious condition. She suffered from shock and severe lacerations of the face and scalp and died the evening of December 24.

Robert C. Quinn, an assistant postal superintendent who was a passenger on the trolley, described the accident. **William H. Kreiling,**

civil engineer, provided details about the tunnel's construction and surroundings. **Harold Mariska**, the bartender at the Hotel Brandt, confirmed that the motorman was in the hotel's bar room at 12:30 p.m. on the day of the accident and was served a glass of beer and a shot of whiskey. And **Deputy Coroner Samuel Shenken** reported on the outcome of the coroner's inquest.

City detective **Charles Freeborn**, an important witness for the commonwealth, testified that after the trolley was replaced, the car sprang forward and continued through the tunnel; "the further in it went, the faster it went and when it struck the curb outside the tunnel it turned over." Despite the defense attorney's objections concerning the witness's qualifications, Freeborn estimated that the car was going fifty to sixty miles per hour when it was about five hundred feet from the north end of the tunnel. He said he frequently rode through the tunnel on a streetcar and could judge the speed of the car because there was enough light to see inside the tunnel and inside the car. In addition, he reported that he had once chased some payroll robbers in an automobile on the Boulevard of the Allies traveling sixty miles per hour. Freeborn confirmed the car had side entry doors and a conductor's cash box in the center of the car. Before the wreck, he said he was standing near the cash box. During the crash, he was ejected from the car, thrown across Carson Street and landed on the pavement in the front of the car. Freeborn also stated that the rear end of the car was splintered when it hit the poles and turned over.

Locomotive engineer **H.B. Carroll** was standing within two feet of the motorman when the trolley wrecked. Carroll provided the most damaging testimony against Klingler. He stated that the car after going fifty to fifty-five miles per hour through the tunnel was traveling thirty-five miles per hour when it left the tracks at the north end of the tunnel. Someone had given the two-bell signal after the trolley was replaced, and the car started off with a jerk. The motorman turned the controller all the way around. It was wide open at full speed. The first thing he noticed was that the car started to rock and then he realized it was going very fast. He said, "The lights on the side of the tunnel began to shoot by. Then I looked again at the controller and saw that it was still wide open. Just as I was going to say something to the motorman about it, he shut it off. We were about 500 feet from the entrance of the tunnel. He then applied the brakes." During cross examination, Carroll did not waver. Carroll said he "was not injured until the car came to a dead stop and the persons remaining in the front of the car were hurled against him. He was stunned but not rendered unconscious."

The state rested its case against Klingler on February 12 after calling **A.D. Neeld**, civil engineer and Mount Washington Tunnel designer, and Deputy Coroner **George Ambos**. Neeld confirmed that the tunnel had a grade of 5.86 percent for all but the first one hundred feet at the south end. Ambos saw the motorman at South Side Hospital after the accident and stated that Klingler said he had been drinking before the accident.

The defense presented only a few witnesses. The first was a Knoxville street cleaner, **John Fitzsimmons**, who reportedly heard a cracking sound when the car passed him on Amanda Street. He found a brake shoe lying on the pavement. The prosecution then called **Frank R. Phillips**, a Pittsburgh Railways engineer, who testified that the brake Fitzsimmons found would not have fit on the car that wrecked. Phillips added that he examined the car after the accident and found all of the brakes intact and operational.

Motorman Klingler took the stand in his own defense and admitted to having several drinks on the day of the accident but denied being intoxicated. Klingler had not slept the night before the accident. He said prior to the wreck he used "ordinary precaution, but when he was halfway through the tunnel he noticed the car was going fast and applied the air brakes. They refused to respond, he said, and then he reversed the controller and applied the hand brake but the car continued in its flight."

Several character witnesses testified that Klingler was a "careful man." His father, **George Klingler**, said he saw his son the day of the accident, and he was not intoxicated.

Witness testimony ended at 3:00 p.m. on February 12. Both attorneys presented their closing arguments, and the judge charged the jury the next day.

Attorney Brennen spoke first. He contended that the state had not proven beyond a reasonable doubt that Klingler's negligence caused the accident and said that it was immaterial whether Klingler was sober or not, unless Klingler was responsible for the wreck. And he said that it didn't matter if Klingler was drunk if he did what was necessary to properly operate the trolley and tried to keep it under control as it ran through the tunnel. Brennen also attempted to discredit the testimony of prosecution witnesses who estimated the car was going fifty to sixty miles per hour. He said Carroll and Freeborn were wrong and the error called into question their entire testimony. Brennen claimed trains running in open areas seldom attain such speeds and that it was technically impossible for a streetcar traveling through a tunnel to go that fast.

Assistant District Attorney Estep then summarized the evidence against Klingler:

The Commonwealth's case rests upon these declarations: that Klingler was not in a condition to operate a car, as on the night of December 23 he visited a downtown club, where he drank whiskey and never went to bed at all that night; that when he reported to work that the night dispatcher refused to assign him to a run and that he was later given one by the day dispatcher; that after making several trips he went to his brother's butcher shop, where he had some liquor, drinking whiskey and beer; and afterwards got more drink at a saloon; that he operated his car recklessly, turning the controller on full while going through the tunnel with its steep grade and that at the time the accident occurred his car was running from 50 to 60 miles per hour. It is upon these allegations that the Commonwealth will ask for a conviction.

Court documents indicate that Brennen made a series of arguments to the judge about what should be included in his charge to the jury before deliberations began. He urged that the jury be instructed not to consider the totality of the accident or that twenty-three people died and over eighty were injured. The judge refused this request and several others, including instructing the jury to not consider intoxication as a factor if the motorman had done all that a sober person would have done to avoid or mitigate the accident or take into account speed as a factor if the motorman did all that he could to avoid the accident. In addition, Brennen stated that overcrowding of the car was unusual, and the motorman had the right to depend on the conductor to operate the emergency brake inside the car if the speed of the car was high and dangerous.

Shortly after the lunch break on February 13, Judge Swearingen instructed the jury. The judge emphasized that "the defendant is not on trial for being drunk, but the testimony on that point is relevant as bearing on the ultimate question of whether or not he performed his duties as motorman as a reasonably prudent and careful man would have done under the circumstances." He also said that the case was presented with extreme care and that the careful arguments relieved the court of "having to recount the evidence in detail." The jury began deliberations at 2:20 p.m.

The jury deliberated for almost an hour and returned a verdict at 3:15 p.m. Foreman Albert Edge reported the jury had found H.H. Klingler guilty on two counts in the deaths of Clara Tanney and Ella C. Sheridan and not guilty in the death of Gladys H. Sheridan.

Standing before the court, Klingler, expecting to be acquitted on all charges, appeared shocked by the verdict. He turned pale and nearly collapsed. Attorney Brennen helped him back into his seat.

Reprint from Pittsburg Press, *February 13, 1919.*

Judge Swearingen then explained that when charging the jury, he had directed the jurors to find the defendant not guilty on the indictment related to Gladys H. Sheridan because the commonwealth could not clearly demonstrate that she died as a result of injuries sustained in the accident. The doctor who cared for her was in the U.S. Army stationed in France and was unable to testify at the trial. Although it was confirmed that Sheridan was a passenger on the car when it wrecked and her injuries were sufficiently serious to require hospitalization, according to the rules of evidence, hospital records were not admissible in making a case for involuntary manslaughter. The jury, in its verdict, recommended the mercy of the court be exercised when sentencing the defendant.

After the verdict was rendered, Assistant District Attorney Estep indicated that Klingler would be called for trial on the twenty other charges of involuntary manslaughter in the near future. Klingler remained out on bail until he was sentenced.

MOTION FOR NEW TRIAL

Within days of Klingler's conviction, his attorney filed a motion for a new trial, citing that errors committed by Judge Swearingen led to errors in the trial's outcome. In his motion, Brennen reiterated the points he had previously made to the judge. He questioned the court's judgment in permitting the prosecution of only three of twenty-three indictments against Klingler, allowing a witness to estimate the car's speed as it traveled through the tunnel, permitting the jury to consider whether a motorman with an understanding of his job responsibilities would knowingly drink liquor before taking over a streetcar and relying on carelessness rather than gross negligence to form the basis for an involuntary manslaughter conviction.

On July 3, 1919, after hearing oral arguments and considering the motion, Judge Joseph H. Swearingen and Judge J.J. Stone refused to grant the defendant's motion for a new trial. The jury's decision to convict H.H. Klingler in February 1919 for involuntary manslaughter in the deaths of Clara Tanney and Ella C. Sheridan and acquit him in the death of Gladys H. Sheridan would stand.

The court also stated that it was the prosecutor's prerogative to try only three of twenty-three charges, as there was no legal mandate requiring all charges be tried at one time. They noted that this objection, raised at the beginning of the trial, had been denied.

The judges also said that an involuntary manslaughter conviction recognized the failure to perform a legal duty to safeguard human life and is justified when death was unintentional and resulted from an unlawful act or lawful act done in an unlawful manner. Nowhere in the law was there a requirement that a defendant to be found guilty of gross negligence, the deliberate and reckless disregard for the safety or others, in order to be found guilty of involuntary manslaughter. The actions by the defendant to reduce the speed of the car were too late, and the car was already beyond control. The motorman's carelessness in running the car without due caution caused the accident and was sufficient to find guilt.

They also found the argument against allowing a witness to assess the speed of the car as it traveled through the tunnel had no merit. The witnesses, through their experiences riding through the tunnel for years, knew what the average speed was and could distinguish the difference in speed prior to the trolley wreck. One of the witnesses, a Knoxville resident and P&LE locomotive engineer for fifteen years, rode both the locomotive and trolley on a daily basis and was qualified and within his legal rights to assess the trolley's speed.

In addition, the court believed the issue of inebriation could not be removed from the jury's consideration. Klingler's actions were not normal, and "his position as motorman required such care and judgment that if a man, knowing this fact, deliberately became intoxicated, then assumes these duties, it is certainly evidence for the jury." The court then questioned whether a "reasonably prudent man...a sober man" would have "started the trolley with violent jerk by throwing off the brakes and throwing on full power...until the speed attained was so great he had lost all control of it... before attempting to stop the trolley."

Sentencing

Six months after conviction, Judge Swearingen sentenced Klingler to a minimum of fifteen months and not more than two years in the Western Penitentiary on two counts of involuntary manslaughter. The sentences would run concurrently. He was also ordered to pay a fine of 6¼ cents to the commonwealth, a value generally associated with being treated as a pauper in Allegheny County.

Klingler entered prison on July 12, 1919. He was released from Western Penitentiary on October 10, 1920, after serving the minimum of a fifteen to twenty-four-month sentence.

In September 1920, Allegheny County district attorney Harry H. Rowand petitioned Common Pleas Court for the final disposition of the remaining twenty involuntary manslaughter indictments against H.H. Klinger. Chief Clerk George Connor placed the cases on the criminal court trial list for final disposition either by pleas of guilty by the defendant or motions to nolle prosequi by the district attorney.

Klingler's attorney, William J. Brennen, responded to the district attorney's petition with a plea of autrefois convict, arguing that his client could not be

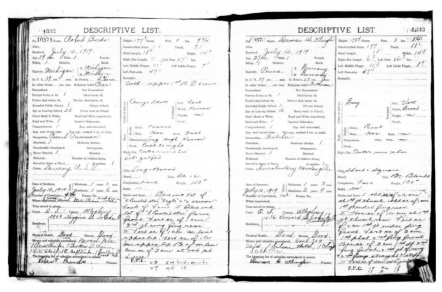

Western Penitentiary, descriptive list, page 1,233. Entry for Herman H. Klinger. *Pennsylvania Historical and Museum Commission, Harrisburg, Pennsylvania, Population Records: Descriptive Lists, Series: 15.128.*

Western Penitentiary Herman H. Klingler identification card. *Pennsylvania Historical and Museum Commission, Harrisburg, Pennsylvania, Prisoner Fingerprint Identification Cards, Series:15.139.*

tried for an offense if he had previously been convicted for the same offense. Brennen claimed that Klingler could not be tried for deaths occurring in the same place at the same time and by the same act or acts caused by negligence or otherwise. He said that Klingler was at that time serving a sentence in the Western Penitentiary for his conviction on two of three charges of like nature. He further contended that the evidence in support of the state's case would not differ from that which formed the basis for his prior conviction.

On September 20, 1920, after assistant district attorney agreed with Brennen's rationale, Judge John A. Evans directed the jury hearing the case to find a verdict in favor of the defense's plea. The jury acted in accordance with the directive, and jury foreman Jon M. Lindsay reported that the "defendant had been convicted heretofore on the charges named in the above indictments, Nos. 46, 48, 50, 52, 54, 58, 60, 62, 64, 66, 68, 72, 74, 76, 78, 80, 82, 84, 86, 90," identifying the twenty indictments by their reference numbers. Judge Evans then struck the twenty indictments for involuntary manslaughter from the docket.

CHARGES DROPPED AGAINST DISPATCHER

In March 1918, Michael F. Maley, the Pittsburgh Railways Co. dispatcher, was indicted by a grand jury as an accessory before the fact in the deaths of twenty-three passengers on Knoxville #4236. The district attorney, on February 2, 1923, petitioned the court to drop all charges against Maley, and the court ordered the record cleared.

AFTERNOTES

Herman Henry Klingler, born May 4, 1892, was the son of early 1880s German immigrants George and Elizabeth Erk Klingler. In December 1917, Klingler resided at 16 Carson Street, was single and had worked for Pittsburgh Railways as a motorman for six months. He left school at age sixteen and was a cow puncher in Texas prior to 1917.

Klingler served his sentence at the Western State Penitentiary in Pittsburgh from July 12, 1919, through October 10, 1920. After his release from prison, he lived at 1636 Concordia Street, Carrick, and worked as a butcher. At the time of his death on November 14, 1964, at age seventy-two, he lived in Karns City, Butler County, Pennsylvania. He is buried at South Side Cemetery.

Hamilton "H.B." Carroll, a critical figure in the criminal proceedings, stood within two feet of the motorman when the car went out of control. His testimony described the motorman's operation of the trolley and estimated the car's speed at fifty to sixty miles per hour as it raced through the tunnel and crashed onto Carson Street.

At the time of the accident, Carroll resided at 218 Zara Street, Knoxville, with his wife, Mayme (Armstrong), and three young children: Clark, Gordon and Catherine. As a locomotive engineer employed by the Pittsburgh & Lake

Erie Railroad Co., and based in McKees Rocks, he was likely a frequent Knoxville trolley passenger. By the end of 1925, per the local Presbyterian church records, the Carroll family moved to 1119 Sixth Street, Beaver Borough, where he worked as a P&LE engineer, grocery salesmen, an airplane propeller manufacturer at Curtis-Wright Corp. and a firefighter.

Local newspapers and Allegheny County Coroner's Office records indicate that H.B. Carroll, age sixty-two, died after leaping from the center pier of the fifty-foot-high Smithfield Street bridge at 7:00 p.m. on Wednesday, January 13, 1947. James J. Torick of McKees Rocks, as he was driving across the bridge, saw him and told patrolman John Ramos, who was directing traffic near the bridge. Pittsburgh Police river patrolmen Alexander Ruczka, Lieutenant George Tully and Martin Morgan found his body at 1:10 p.m. the next day in the center of the Monongahela River, about one hundred feet west of the bridge. Carroll was identified by the Social Security card in his pocket.

Carroll's son Gordon Carroll reported that his father, a retired firefighter who had been in ill health for several years, left Beaver County in 1946 and was thought to be living in California with his brother Dr. Charles Carroll. The coroner's inquest held on January 28, 1947, determined that death was due to drowning. Carroll, a native of West Alexander, Washington County, Pennsylvania, was the son of H.B. and Ida May (Underwood) Carroll.

9

CIVIL CLAIMS ARISING FROM
DECEMBER 24, 1917 TUNNEL ACCIDENT

Within weeks of the accident, Knoxville #4236 victims and their families filed the first civil suits as actions at trespass against the Pittsburgh Railways Co. The *Pittsburgh Chronicle* reported that W.D. Grimes, the former Knoxville Borough solicitor, filed the first two petitions on behalf of Phillip J. and Edna M. Fischer and Coleman and Nora Flaherty on January 9, 1918. Both sought damages of $15,000 for injuries suffered by the women. Grimes alleged that the Pittsburgh Railways Co. was negligent when it permitted the overcrowding of the streetcar and allowed an inexperienced, careless and intoxicated motorman to operate it. The claims were rooted in the rationale that when a passenger paid a fare, it became a contract with Pittsburgh Railways to provide safe carriage. And when the motorman ran the trolley at an excessive, unsafe speed through the tunnel and passengers were killed or injured, that contract was broken.

Allegheny County Common Pleas Court records indicate that victims or their families filed at least seventy civil suits against the Pittsburgh Railways Co.; forty-eight were filed in 1918, sixteen in 1919 and six in 1920. Victims and, in many cases, men on behalf of their wives and/or children sought compensation for medical expenses, lost wages due to temporary or permanent physical or mental disability and pain and suffering, as well as reimbursement for lost or damaged personal property. The accident's effect on women was accentuated by their husbands' demands for reimbursement for the costs of services necessitated by the loss of a mother's capacity to care for children or a wife's ability to maintain a household. Claims for funeral expenses were made for all who died except Josephine Retzback, Clara Miller and Pauline Dewmyer.

Demands for tens of thousands of dollars in damages and costs were sought. All of the petitioners requested jury trials, perhaps with an eye to the potential for having decisions made by members of the larger community that so profoundly felt the impact of the accident. The Pittsburgh Railways Co., prior to the first trial, accepted liability for the accident. Subsequent Civil Court proceedings then focused on establishing the company's level of financial responsibility to the victims and their families. From available records, compensation claims for forty-one of the seventy cases exceeded $1.1 million. Twenty-nine attorneys represented seventy victims, with prominent Pittsburgh attorney H. Fred Mercer acting on behalf of nine.

PHYSICAL AND MENTAL ANGUISH

According to the details in the court filings, victims and their families suffered great physical pain and mental anguish in the weeks, months and, in some instances, years following the accident. The nature and extent of the injuries were significant. Fractured skulls; facial cuts; neck, back and spine sprains; arm, shoulder, rib, pelvis and leg fractures; chest and abdominal injuries; and the loss of sight, hearing and teeth often caused permanent physical incapacity and disfigurement. Shock, nervousness, sleeplessness and "weak mindedness" described the mental distress experienced by many. Weeks and months of hospitalization and/or in-home care were frequently documented, with over half of the victims expressing a need for future short or long-term medical treatment.

The petitions also provide details about the accident. James Leonard reported that he was violently thrown from his position in the car, knocked down, tramped on and struck by debris and wreckage. Viola Butler recounted that she was jarred, jolted, struck, dragged and permanently disabled after suffering head injuries that required three surgeries and a partial removal of her skull.

The long-term effects of the accident were also revealed in the petitions. Mollie Belz, a saleswoman from West Virginia, was described as "greatly disfigured." Caroline Young Barrett's right side was partially paralyzed. Teresa Gorman, after being crushed in the accident and spending fourteen weeks in the hospital, was deemed permanently and hopelessly crippled and likely unable to perform labor for the rest of her life. Elmer Rushway lost his wife, Clara, as well as their unborn child. Mabel Brecht's husband simply stated that "the children lost their mother."

Later, in court testimony, Etra DeMartini, recounted that she was on the left side of the car as it exited the tunnel, in the second seat from the conductor. When the car overturned, she fell between the seats, and others fell on top of her. In addition to multiple injuries to the right side of her body, she experienced continuous headaches, feared traveling in a vehicle and suffered from sleeplessness and crying fits. According to two neighbors who testified, DeMartini was unable to take care of her home and family.

As noted earlier, not all of the victims were passengers. Others in the vicinity of Carson and Smithfield Street were injured when the trolley crashed and slid through the intersection.

George Birmingham, age thirty-eight, emigrated from Ireland in 1893 and worked as an express wagon driver in Pittsburgh. He stated that he was a passenger on a wagon traveling in an easterly direction on Carson Street. When the horse and wagon reached the streetcar tracks that extended from the north end of the tunnel toward the Smithfield Street Bridge, the driver, with due care and caution, started across the streetcar tracks. The trolley "came northbound from the tunnel at great rate of speed across Carson Street, struck the horse and wagon and injured him." In addition to a permanently damaged left leg, he suffered internal injuries and injuries to his back, both arms, right hip and head. His World War I draft card issued in September 1918 indicated one leg was shorter than the other. The wagon's driver, Morris Julius, was not injured; the horse died.

Tomys Kahnych, age thirty-three, an early 1900s immigrant from Austria-Hungary, was standing on the sidewalk at the corner of Smithfield and Carson Streets. The trolley hit him when it slid on its side and up on to the sidewalk at the northwest corner of the intersection. Kahnych was struck with such force and violence that he was hurled to the ground. He was rendered unconscious and remained so for several hours. He spent four weeks in South Side Hospital recovering from a fractured pelvis and brain, kidney, spine and hip injuries. The Carnegie Steel Co. employee lost two months of work and bore permanent facial and hand scars.

"EXCESSIVE" JURY VERDICTS

Although court records are generally sparse, there is clear evidence that the Pittsburgh Railways Co. objected to the jury verdicts and routinely sought new trials, citing "excessive" compensation for medical expenses, lost wages or diminished earnings capacity, physical impairments, pain and suffering. The company's aggressive responses to the jury verdicts can be seen in trial transcripts and court decisions published in the *Pittsburgh Legal Journal*. A comparison of the jury verdicts to accident-related claims against the Pittsburgh Railways Co. outstanding in 1922 indicates the company's efforts met with little success. The courts let all of the jury verdicts stand.

Superior Court challenges by the Pittsburgh Railways Co. to verdicts in favor of Margaret M. Miller, William R. Bolitho and the Rosenberger family are a window into the company's actions to minimize its financial responsibility to the victims and their families.

In 1921, the *Pittsburgh Legal Journal* reported **Margaret M. Miller**'s case as one of the "tunnel cases" growing out of the running away and overturning of a heavily loaded streetcar near the mouth of the Mount Washington Tunnel in the city of Pittsburgh on December 24, 1917. Miller, age thirty-one, the wife of Albert A. Miller, a local newspaper employee, suffered the total loss of use of her left arm. A jury in March 1920 awarded the Knoxville couple a combined verdict of $22,000. The Pittsburgh Railways Co. requested a new trial, citing four reasons: the verdicts were grossly excessive; the verdicts were against the weight of the evidence; the court erred in instructing the jury on the measure of damages relating to humiliation, distress of mind, et cetera; and the court erred in allowing the jury to guess the expense of a future operation that might be performed on Miller's hand and arm. On June 30, 1920, a three-judge panel, Judges John A. Evans, Ambrose B. Reid and Charles H. Kline, denied all four arguments made by the Pittsburgh Railways Co., stating that the verdict was not excessive, and refused the motion for a new trial.

Judge Reid, writing for the court, stated:

> *Mrs. Miller was very seriously hurt as the result of the accident. She was confined to St. Joseph's Hospital for three months; when removed to her home, she was in bed for three weeks; and for a year afterwards was, as she described it, "sick and dragging." Her nerves were affected; she was unable to sleep, and suffered pain all of that time. Her principal injury, however, was to her left hand, which had been so terribly hurt and deformed that the*

Sisters Were Passengers; One Dead; Other Injured

Mrs A A Miller

Mrs E G Rushway

An all-day search for two Knoxville sisters ended at 1 o'clock this morning with discovery of one in the morgue and the other in St Joseph's Hospital. Their husbands believed they boarded the fatal Knoxville car yesterday afternoon, but it was not until late last night that Albert A Miller, 233 Arabella street, Knoxville, found his wife injured, being treated for a cut and bruised arm and minor injuries. As for Elmer G Rushway, 217 Arabella street, Knoxville, he refused to believe that any of the bodies in the morgue was that of his wife until this morning, when her identity was proved. Mrs Miller was formerly Miss Margaret Delaney. Mr Miller is a member of the business office force of The Dispatch.

Clara B. Rushway and her sister, Margaret Miller, lived on Arabella Street, Knoxville, and were passengers on the Knoxville trolley. Rushway died in the accident, and Miller was seriously injured. *Reprint from* Pittsburg Dispatch, *December 25, 1917.*

attending surgeon did not wish her to look at it for weeks after the accident. The sight of this hand, scarred and discolored, with the fingers all drawn into the wrist, a shapeless and repelling object, the result of the accident, no doubt had great weight in influencing the jury to find a very generous verdict—one which defendants' counsel term "excessive." It was not only the crippled and unsightly condition of this hand for which the jurors sought to compensate the plaintiff, but for the long and trying hospital experience which she underwent in the efforts of the surgeon not only to save her hand, but her life.

The plaintiff's and defendant's attorneys—H. Fred Mercer and Walter M. Lindsey, respectively—relied on medical professionals to provide expert opinion about Miller's long-term diagnosis. Her attending physician, Dr. Richard J. Behan, characterized as capable and reputable by the jurist, described Miller's injuries and treatment in his testimony. He stated that "the skin was cut through and the tissues beneath were lacerated and torn; the wound was repaired, but infection set in and the patient was dangerously ill for three weeks, and the blood poisoning affected her whole system, and in order to save her life there were several transfusions of blood. The infection spread up the arm into the tendon sheathes, and it was necessary to twice open those sheathes and the pockets of pus in order to relieve the patient and finally effect a cure." The doctor thought there was some movement in the fingers and that the appearance of the hand and its usefulness could be improved by another operation.

Dr. Harold Ralston, in describing present circumstances, thought the appearance of Miller's hand could be improved, but not the movement. "The hand as it is will never be better….She can't use the hand any more than if it was practically amputated."

In response, doctors on behalf of Pittsburgh Railways presented a more optimistic view. Dr. John Purman admitted, "At present the hand is a useless member. As time goes on, her nervous condition will improve, and if her hand was well, it [the nervous condition] would clear up entirely. An operation removing the scar tissue would put it in perfect shape, so that there would be no deformity, and this would to a considerable extent restore the functioning of the hand. It would never become a perfectly useful hand."

Dr. Joseph M. Jackson testified "that the appearance of the hand can be greatly improved and its normal function largely restored by an operation. The improved appearance would result in overcoming the nervousness and embarrassment from which the plaintiff suffers." Dr. Jackson described that the repair of Miller's hand would involve removing the scar tissue and then opening a "flap" or pocket in the flesh of the patient's thigh, where the hand would be held rigidly in place by putting the arm in a plaster of Paris cast for three weeks and would grow new skin.

Judge Reid then observed that the jury had undoubtedly considered Dr. Jackson's testimony and wrote, "Such treatment, if submitted to, involves more pain and suffering on the part of the wife and more expenditure on the part of the husband. The very description of the proposed operation helped to increase the amount of the verdict....the jury had to determine the whole question, and may well have found that there was no assurance that any amount of surgery and of further pain, suffering, and expense would be certain of effecting a cure and restoring that which the plaintiff had lost through the defendant's negligence—a slightly, normal and useful left hand."

Continuing, the judge wrote, "Mrs. Miller is thirty-one years of age, of apparent refinement and good appearance. She was in good health before the accident, and able to do all the household work which a willing and healthy wife could do. In considering the question of the reasonableness or excessiveness of the verdicts, it is important to bear in mind the comparative youth of the injured woman and the consequent likelihood of her suffering for many years to come, and of her husband's being, to a great extent, deprived of her wifely services for an equally long time."

The judge ended by suggesting that it might have been better had Miller's hand been amputated and that for purposes of compensation, the jurors evidently viewed the loss of the hand as final. "Under all the circumstances, although the verdicts may seem large, they are not so large as to shock the judicial conscience."

William R. Bolitho, a thirty-year-old Knoxville resident, died at Mercy Hospital of shock and hemorrhaging several hours after the trolley accident. At the time of his death, he was a sheet metal worker and earned $140 per month, with $100 allocated to the support of his wife and child. His widow, Amelia Bolitho, in her suit against the Pittsburgh Railways Co., sought compensation for the loss of her husband and support of William Jr., their sixteen-month-old son. William had recently completed studies and qualified as a heating and ventilating engineer and expected in the spring of 1918 to engage in a different line of work. A jury verdict in November 1919 awarded Amelia $12,785. On December 29, 1919, the Pittsburgh Railways Co. filed a motion for a new trial, alleging that the verdict was excessive.

William R. Bolitho, a naturalized citizen, emigrated from England as a child, in 1896, with his mother, Jane, and five siblings, Thomas, Mary, Eva, Hetty and James. Public records suggest that they joined Thomas Bolitho, their husband and father, who had previously settled in Pittsburgh.

The Pittsburgh Railways Co. motion was heard by a three-judge panel, Judges James R. MacFarlane, Thomas J. Ford and Stephen Stone. George P.

TREE THERE, SPIRIT MISSING;
MOTHER AND SISTER INJURED

Left to Right, Mrs. Christina Rosenberger, Henry Rosenberger
and Miss Elfreda Rosenberger.

William H. Bolitho, Wife and Child

Left: The William Bolitho family. *Reprint from* Pittsburg Dispatch, *December 26, 1917.*

Above: Christina Rosenberger, Henry Rosenberger and Elfreda Rosenberger. *Reprint from* Gazette Times, *December 26, 1917.*

Kountz represented Amelia Bolitho, while R.L. Long advocated on behalf of the Pittsburgh Railways Co.

Judge Stone, writing for the court on December 29, 1919, stated, "[A] verdict of $12,785.00 was not excessive where a husband, aged 30 years, was killed, having in mind decedent's age, his condition of health, the money he was making at the time of the accident, his studious habits, the amount the plaintiff used for herself and her children, the wife being about 30-years old at the time of the accident and in good health." Given the circumstances, "we are not convinced the verdict as rendered by the jury was excessive and the motion for a new trial must therefore be refused."

The most detailed court records involve **Christina Rosenberger**, age thirty-six, and her two children **Elfreda**, age twenty-two, and **Henry**, age twelve. Elfreda Rosenberger was on her way to work the 5:00 p.m. shift as a Bell Telephone operator. She, her mother and brother boarded the trolley near their Hobart Street home in Knoxville. All sustained significant injuries. Separate jury trials were held in early 1920. Christina Rosenberger's case against the Pittsburgh Railways Co. was the first. Christina Schwenning was the second wife and widow of Carl Rosenberger. Carl died in 1910 and left her with nine children aged three to twenty-two years old—Francis, Helen, Henry O., Johanna C., Ernest J., Carl W., Albert, Louisa and Elfreda. The two eldest were her stepchildren. For five years prior to the accident, she was the sole provider for her family. She worked as a seamstress and earned $35 per week. She sought $50,000 to compensate for medical and surgical expenses and her impaired earnings capacity. Three years after the accident, she was still unable to lift her left leg or use her left arm. Federal census records from 1920 support her contention, as eight of Christina's children, Carl, Henry, Louisa, Elfreda, Francis, Johanna, Helen and Ernest, are listed as part of the Chester and Alberta Rosenberger household on Meridian Street, Mount Washington. There is no mention of Christina. The jury on January 21, 1920, awarded her $17,500. On January 23, 1920, attorneys for the Pittsburgh Railways Co. petitioned for a new trial, alleging that the verdict was excessive. A three-judge panel, John A. Evans, Marshall Brown and James B. Drew, did not agree and denied the request on May 25, 1920.

Judge Drew, writing for the court, stated that Christina was painfully and permanently injured due to the negligence of the Pittsburgh Railways Co. "She suffered fractures of the hip joint and the transverse process of the fifth and sixth vertebrae and an injury to the muscles and nerves of her hand." Physicians on both sides agreed "that she has suffered a permanent injury to her leg, which renders the leg almost wholly useless. The condition of her arm may improve, but it now seems unlikely that there will be a complete recovery. She has been forced to undergo great pain and inconvenience and will be, to a large extent, so afflicted in the future….Her earning power has been damaged or destroyed. For these reasons, and because she was in good health and but thirty-six years of age at the time of the accident, we are of the opinion that the verdict of $17,500, cannot fairly be said to be excessive. Motion denied and new trial refused."

Henry O. Rosenberger also sustained serious and permanent injuries that affected his back, shoulders, spine, hip, face, head and abdomen. Physical impairments were expected to result in a lifelong diminished earnings capacity. Attorneys sought $40,000—$30,000 for Henry and $10,000 for his mother to pay medical bills. On January 21, 1920, a jury awarded them $11,800. Attorneys for the Pittsburgh Railways Co., on January 23, 1920, requested a new trial, citing the verdict as excessive. In May 1920, the court denied the request.

Elfreda Rosenberger had worked seven years as an operator for Bell Telephone. At the time of the accident, as the chief night operator, she earned $16.50 per week. Like other victims, she accumulated medical bills and lost wages. Her injuries were numerous and affected many parts of her body. The right side of her face was cut, deformed and mashed. She was in a coma for ten days and had no recollection of the accident.

The muscles, nerves and ligaments of her arms and hands were damaged. The little finger on her left hand was torn from the knuckle to her wrist She suffered a concussion, impaired eyesight and lost four upper teeth. The civil court petition filed by H. Fred Mercer on her behalf sought $50,000 in compensation and damages. On March 2, 1920, the jury returned a verdict of $10,000. By March 20, 1920, attorneys for the Pittsburgh Railways Co. filed a motion for a new trial due to an excessive verdict and questioned the determination of future earnings.

Greater details about Elfreda's injuries are revealed in the March 3, 1920 Allegheny County Common Pleas Court trial transcript. After being discharged from St. Joseph's Hospital in March 1918, she remained bedridden at home for four to five weeks. A doctor visited her home six or seven times per day until April 1918 to remove glass fragments from her face and check on the eight facial drains used to draw off infection. Medical expenses of $655 listed in-home nursing care for five weeks at a cost of $100, $474 for the surgeon, $79 for dental work and $2 for X-rays. Elfreda's lost wages for twenty-four weeks were estimated at $396. The total cost, without consideration for loss of future earnings capacity, was $1,051, far in excess of the $858 she earned in one year.

Facial scarring became the major point of disagreement during the trial. Pictures of the scars were shown to the jury. Elfreda's attending physician, Dr. Benjamin L. Adler, stated that the large, disfiguring scars near her mouth and forehead had not gotten better in eighteen months and were not likely to get better in the next eighteen years.

Dr. Joseph Jackson, testifying on behalf of the Pittsburgh Railways Co., stated that "the scars of the face were disfiguring scars as far as appearance is concerned, but they are not scars that interfered with the function…any of the functions of the face…any of the muscles of the face….The scars seemed to be limited to the superficial tissues and were not fastened or bound in any way, so the movements of the face and mouth and eyes were not interfered with….Not disability scars."

Newspapers at the time reported that the Pittsburgh Railways Co. attorneys used before-and-after accident photographs of Elfreda Rosenberger to argue that she wasn't very attractive before the accident and that her injuries didn't diminish her appearance afterward.

A three-judge panel, John A. Evans, Ambrose B. Reid and Charles H. Kline, heard the motion for a new trial. Judge Kline, writing for the court on May 26, 1920, stated, "[The] picture exhibited at trial showed much disfigurement of the face, that there was much mental in addition to the physical suffering endured by the plaintiff by virtue of the accident and will be continued to be endured. In addition, violent headaches affect her ability to work and she has a continual flow of saliva due to an injury to the carotid glands....We are of the opinion that the verdict is not excessive and evidence was sufficient for jury to determine whether future earnings would be affected. Motion for new trial was refused."

OUTCOMES

The first trials occurred in early 1919, the last in 1924. Verdicts totaling $288,198.54 were returned by juries in fifty-four cases. Morris Julius and the families of Howard Ford and Adele Bongiovanni settled with the Pittsburgh Railways Co. through arbitration. Lack of appearance by eight petitioners resulted in the court's dismissal of those cases. Two of the dismissals related to Leopold Czerny, who had moved to Detroit, and Caroline Barrett Young, who had passed away. Five additional cases were listed in court indices, but no further record of their outcome is available.

THE PITTSBURGH RAILWAYS CO. BANKRUPTCY, 1918

CREDITORS FORCE RECEIVERSHIP

By early 1918, the Philadelphia Company, the parent company of the Pittsburgh Railways Co., had evolved into a financing and supervisory agent for a variety of profitable oil, gas, coal, electric and transportation concerns. According to its *34th Annual Report to Shareholders*, the company controlled eighteen separate entities, including Allegheny Steam Heating Co., Mount Washington Street Railway, Duquesne Light Co., Equitable Gas Co., Equitable Coke, Equitable Coal, Allegheny Valley Railroad, Harmony Railroad, Beaver Valley Traction Co., Pittsburgh and Beaver Street Railway Co., Clairton Street Railway Co., Monongahela Natural Gas, Pittsburgh West Virginia Gas Co., Philadelphia Oil Co., Beaver County Light Co., Diamond Light and Power Co., Midland Electric Light and Power Co. and the Mount Washington Transit Tunnel. There was no mention of the Pittsburgh Railways Co. Instead, a December 31, 1917 interim report stated that "no earnings from the Pittsburgh Railways Co. are included in this report, as receivers were appointed for that Company, on April 23, 1918, by the District Court of the United States for the Western District of Pennsylvania."

On January 1, 1918, the Pittsburgh Railways Co. failed to pay the principal and interest due on outstanding long-term debt.

A group of Pittsburgh Railways Co. bondholders sharply criticized the Philadelphia Company for defaulting on its debt payment and its practice of isolating the financial responsibility for the Pittsburgh Railways Co. from the rest of the Philadelphia Company's assets. The absence of information about the profitability of the Pittsburgh Railways Company's underlying traction companies also caused significant concern. The group urged collective action to ensure the continued operation of the trolley system, the enforcement of bondholders' rights and to secure the cooperation of the City of Pittsburgh to protect the interests of the traveling public. The *Evening Public Ledger* on January 4, 1918, reported the Mount Washington trolley accident and anticipated victim damage claims motivated the non-payment of interest on the Pittsburgh Railways Co. debt and suggested that the Philadelphia Company would use the default as an opportunity to reorganize under federal bankruptcy law to get out from under the street rail system's high level of debt. On February 14, 1918, the bondholders group sued the Philadelphia Company in federal district court in western Pennsylvania to force payment of the interest due and to cause all of Pittsburgh Railways Co.'s long-term debt to become a lien against the Philadelphia Company

A few months later, on April 22, 1918, attorney George B. Gordon, acting on behalf of the American Brake Shoe and Foundry Co. of Wilmington, Delaware, the St. Louis Car Co. of St. Louis, Missouri, and all creditors wishing to join the suit petitioned the federal district court in Pittsburgh to place the Pittsburgh Railways Co. into receivership. The Pittsburgh Railways Co. owed American Brake Shoe $7,077.35 and the St. Louis Car Co. $2,045.50 for essential materials and supplies. The petitioners described the company's financial situation as a "house of cards" and implied that the failure of the Pittsburgh Railways Co. would cause defaults in its underlying street railway companies. At that time, the company had $41.5 million in total debt and owed another $3.4 million in annual interest and lease payments to its constituent companies. The increasing burden of current and future wage increases was also noted. The petitioners sought a court-appointed receiver to preserve the operation of the transit system and permit the sale of the company's assets to pay outstanding obligations.

Attorney E.W. Smith represented the Pittsburgh Railways Co. During a federal court hearing, Smith admitted financial problems existed and agreed that receivership was appropriate. Newspapers at the time reported that recent fare increases provided sufficient income for the company to operate under normal circumstances, but once the United States entered World War

I in April 1917, available revenue could not keep up with the rapid growth in labor and material costs. Rising operating costs and financial obligations of $9,679,099 for pending civil damage claims, mostly related to the Christmas Eve tunnel disaster, were so onerous that the Pittsburgh Railways Co. was doomed to fiscal failure without the assistance of receivership. Smith also argued that absent the court's intervention, the company's bond holders would likely break up the existing transit system to recover their investments. Such action would result in a great inconvenience to passengers and unnecessary losses to the creditors and the bondholders of Pittsburgh Railways and its underlying companies. Service disruptions and equipment failures due to unusually severe weather during the 1917–18 winter also contributed to the company's financial distress.

City solicitor Stephen Stone, in his statement to the court, requested three receivers be appointed to represent the interests of the company, bond holders and the public. Stone also expressed concern over the financial threat posed by the civil damage suits that had grown out of the tunnel wreck.

On April 23, 1918, the Pittsburgh Railways Co. became a ward of the Western District Court of Pennsylvania. Judges W.H.S. Thomson and C.P. Orr transferred responsibility for 604 miles of track; 1,861 passenger, express and freight cars; and the control of all leases and franchises, stock ownership and operating contracts for over seventy-five underlying street railroad companies to three receivers. H.S.A. Stewart, vice president of Fidelity Title & Trust Co.; Charles A. Fagan, a local attorney and the statewide Democratic Party leader; and J. Dawson Callery, chairman of Board of Directors and former president of the Pittsburgh Railways Co. and the "father of the unified trolley system in Pittsburgh," were appointed by the federal court to maintain service for over 250,000 daily riders and protect the company from making immediate and potentially disastrous settlements with creditors, claimants and bond holders. The receivers were also authorized to set the compensation of all officers, managers and employees and to seek changes to existing franchise agreements. Employees were advised to keep working, and the public was urged to keep riding the streetcars.

Attorney Berne Burns, as representative of the Pennsylvania Public Service Commission, in comments to the court, acknowledged its ongoing investigation of the Pittsburgh Railways Co. service and fare system and requested the receivers' cooperation in determining the underlying value of the Pittsburgh Railways system and establishing a fare structure that was reasonable. He noted that the commission was available and ready to assist the receivers in the execution of their duties.

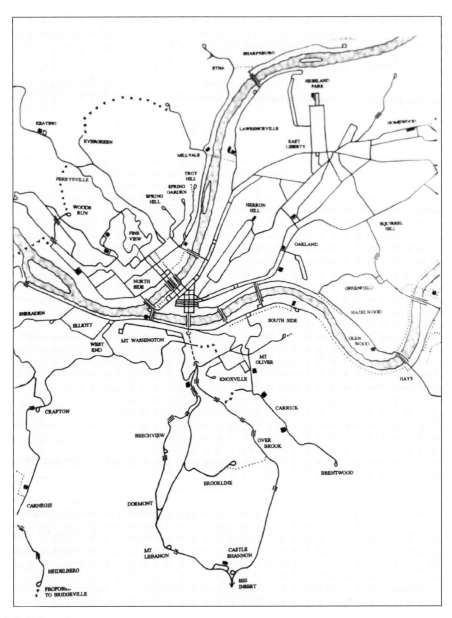

Pittsburgh Railways Co. Service Area as reported by the Pittsburgh Transit Commissioner in 1917. *Courtesy of Archives & Special Collections, University of Pittsburgh Library System.*

In December 1918, after Stewart and Callery resigned, the court appointed S.L. Tone, the president of the Pittsburgh Railways Co., and W.D. George, the federal food administrator for Allegheny County, to act as receivers. With Charles Fagan, they oversaw the company for the next six years. P.W. Jones, Pittsburgh Railways general manager and "Pittsburgh" car designer, managed the company's day-to-day operations.

THE CITY OF PITTSBURGH V. THE PITTSBURGH RAILWAYS CO.

As noted earlier, in 1916, Pittsburgh was the fifth most densely populated city in America. In the twenty years from 1900 to 1920, the city's population grew 53 percent from 321,616 to 588,343 and represented about half of all Allegheny County residents. During the same time, the region's economy was transitioning from glassmaking and mining to becoming the world's leading steel producer. Together, the changes in population and economic activity created a greater demand for more efficient and effective mass transit as motorized vehicles, horses and wagons, streetcars and pedestrians all competed for space on the area's steep and narrow streets.

In late February 1918, several days before the receivership petition was filed, city representatives had been in intense discussions with the Pittsburgh Railways Co. The city's responsibility for transit was established by a state law adopted in 1889 that granted city governments authority to enter into non-locomotive-powered transit franchises. By 1901, the city had awarded an exclusive and perpetual franchise to the Pittsburgh Railways Co. to construct, maintain and operate a street railway in the city for public passenger service. Under the agreement, Pittsburgh Railways had acquired operating rights for over seventy-five street railway companies and controlled three hundred miles of trolley track within the city's borders. Representing the public's interests on fare and service-related concerns and working to maintain or improve city streets to support the transit system became significant concerns for the city. It's involvement in the Pittsburgh Railways Co. bankruptcy proceedings was a natural extension of its ongoing responsibilities under the franchise agreement and transit-related actions the city initiated in 1917. Any changes in the franchise agreement sought by the receivers would have to be approved by the city.

Mayor Edward V. Babcock described the Pittsburgh Railways Company's bankruptcy as "the 'most potent' piece of business that has confronted the mayor and council, the city's legal department and the receivers and others concerned, particularly the public, for the past 20 years." He also predicted that the public would hold him and the city's legal department primarily responsible for safeguarding the interests of the city and public.

In the years preceding the receivership, news reports of passenger complaints were especially acute and focused on service quality, consistency and fares, and the city and railway company's relationship was generally described as contentious. In early 1917, the city appointed E.W. Morse to serve as transit commissioner and employed a staff of engineers and support personnel to investigate the volume and nature of passenger traffic on street railways and steam railroads between the city and adjacent municipalities. In addition, Morse and his group were tasked to study the Pittsburgh Railways Co. routes, rolling stock, track, substations, car barns, operating costs and debt. The city's goal was to determine how to provide rapid, efficient and cheap transit throughout the Pittsburgh region by coordinating public and private efforts. The Pittsburgh Railways Co., citing its status as a private company, refused to participate in the study. Morse and his staff were forced to rely on publicly available reports and citizen surveys to complete their work. The yearlong study, costing over $50,000, was officially released on December 22, 1917.

The Report of the Transit Commissioner indicated that over 165,000 people traveled into the city by trolley each day. System-wide, Pittsburgh Railways' streetcars carried about 277 million passengers per year or about 750,000 per day over 600 miles of track in 2,276 cars for a total of 36.7 million car miles. The average passenger trip inside the city was 2.8 miles and 1.1 miles outside the city limits. A one-way fare in 1917 was five cents.

An analysis of the company's annual financial reports revealed that from 1910 to 1916, Pittsburgh Railways' gross revenue ranged from $10.3 million to $12.6 million per year, while expenses varied from $11.5 million to $11.9 million. From 1910 to 1913, $6.5 million in accumulated operating deficits were funded by bonds issued to the Philadelphia Company From 1914 to 1916, annual operating surpluses averaged close to $1 million each year.

The appendix to the report listed service-related issues. The overcrowding of cars, a factor so apparent in the Knoxville trolley accident, was found to be a frustratingly normal occurrence. Several items described the conditions trolley riders faced each day:

Cars, tracks, and general equipment are poorly maintained, causing accidents and tie-ups that result in poor service. Frequently passengers are requested to leave cars which have broken down and crowd into already overcrowded cars. In addition to this, some of the cars provide uncomfortable riding, because of flat wheels, etc.

In all sections of the city, cars with unfilled seats pass passengers by at stops, when the next car stops, it becomes over filled.

Very large numbers of people crowd into the cars so that in many cars the actual standing room per person is less than 2 sq. feet. Passengers do not object to standing in the street cars in the rush hour, but they do object to being packed in.

Scheduled stop overs at the end of some routes are longer than necessary. Lay-overs should be reduced to provide more service without having to add cars, conductors and motormen. Often the rear platform and back part of cars are described as "very much overcrowded" when, in fact, there is plenty of standing room toward [the] front of the cars. This is partly the fault of employees who don't ask riders to move up front and partly due to riders who don't heed requests. The narrowness of cars with cross seats makes it difficult to move within the car.

Dangerous traffic conditions were also documented. Automobile drivers were observed passing trolleys on both the left and right sides of the cars while passengers attempted to exit or enter cars. Autos stopped too near street corners blocked tracks, causing delays for streetcars trying to make turns. Cars and trucks also parked at trolley stops in violation of traffic laws. Motor vehicles reportedly parked in the central business district on both sides of narrow streets. Construction activity in the city center frequently obstructed streets and trucks and wagons blocked tracks when they are loading or unloading. Wagons parked on the streets at night without lights created a hazard. And, pedestrians didn't heed traffic signals and blocked sidewalks near trolley stops.

To address the issues raised in the report, the Transit Commissioner recommended $20 million in transit system improvements, the widening and reconfiguration of streets and the imposition of new parking regulations. Commissioner Morris also proposed state legislation to permit cities to condemn and take over street railways, create public transit systems and extend lines into unserved areas.

The Pittsburgh Railways Co.'s refusal to participate in the study was generally attributed to its 999-year franchise agreement that left the city with little leverage to independently influence the company. The city's principal recourse then was to seek intervention through the Pennsylvania Public Service Commission, the state's utility oversight authority. On June 29, 1917, the city's solicitor, C.A. O'Brien, filed a general complaint with the commission, alleging that Pittsburgh Railways Co., as the sole provider of street railway transportation in the city, had failed "to furnish reasonably good and sufficient service" and was in violation of Article 2 of the Public Service Company Law. To substantiate the claims, the complaint listed numerous deficiencies related to the traction company's long-term debt, operating methods, management, trolley service, fare and transfer policies and the general condition of its properties and equipment. Citing the Transit Commissioner's preliminary findings, the city also argued that the annual payments made to the Philadelphia Company "on outstanding capital, stock and other securities are unjust, unreasonable and excessive" and were not supportable, given the existing fair valuation of the traction company's physical assets. In other words, the city believed that the Philadelphia Company was profiting from the Pittsburgh Railways Co. at a time when passenger service and the transit system were suffering. The city urged the Public Service Commission to mount a comprehensive investigation of the Pittsburgh Railways Co. and compel remedial actions. In response, the commission created a five-person committee with representatives from the commission, the city and company to examine the charges. That committee met fifty-eight times in the months before April 1918, when the commission issued six orders to Pittsburgh Railways and five recommendations to the city.

The Pittsburgh Railways Co. was not silent during this time. It contended that the city's complaint in 1917, similar to those from 1908, 1909 and 1910, relied on the Public Service Commission to inappropriately force the company to make large expenditures for street improvements. Pittsburgh Railways Co. officials also believed that continued system expansion and improvements were essential to the growth and welfare of the city and urged local officials to cooperate in solving problems and support rather than oppose the company's request to the commission for a fare increase in 1917.

In its annual report to stockholders, dated March 31, 1918, Pittsburgh Railways Co. president S.L. Tone described significant challenges. Tone asserted that the highest number of passenger trips in the company's history occurred in July 1917. Thereafter, passenger trips steadily declined each month as men enlisted or were drafted into military service or those with skills left the area for higher paying, technically oriented

Wanted

Motormen and Conductors

Good positions for men between 19 and 50 years old

Apply 9 to 11 A. M. Daily Except Saturday and Sunday

Employment Office rear 435 Sixth Ave., Pittsburgh

Pittsburgh Railways Co.

Pittsburgh Railways Co. advertised for motormen and conductors to replace those who went into the military or took jobs war related manufacturing. *Reprinted from* Pittsburgh Post, *October 5, 1917.*

government jobs to support the war effort. The company struggled to maintain an adequate workforce and was heartened by the number of women who came forward to undergo training and fill mechanics and maintenance positions. Company officials also believed that women would soon be employed to operate the streetcars. The unexpected changes in the workforce, though, caused the company to operate at its lowest efficiency and pay the highest wages at the same time that the cost of materials and supplies were increasing. He noted that operating costs had risen almost 10 percent or about $1.3 million from April 1917 to March 1918. Two wage increases of 2.5 cents per hour in December 1917 and January 1918 accounted for $875,000 of the added cost. He also alleged that city officials, by discouraging motorman and conductors from working overtime during rush hour, severely affected the company's capacity to provide adequate service.

By the end of April 1918, the receivers acknowledged that the Pittsburgh Railways Co. owed the City of Pittsburgh approximately $380,000 for unpaid taxes, tolls, street improvements and maintenance. On July 20, 1918, the City of Pittsburgh petitioned the federal district court to permit it to intervene in the bankruptcy proceedings on behalf of the city and all interested municipalities. In addition to formalizing its financial claim, the city also sought assurance that the receivers would recognize and understand the problems local governments faced while dealing with the Pittsburgh Railways Co. The court granted the city's petition on November 14, 1918.

PITTSBURGH RAILWAYS RECEIVERSHIP AND KNOXVILLE #4236 TROLLEY ACCIDENT CLAIMS

Although the personal injury and damage claims made by Knoxville #4236 victims or their families were cited as key among the factors that forced the Pittsburgh Railways Co. into receivership, they represented only a portion of the outstanding civil suits against the company. The claims from December 24, 1917 accident were part of a larger and troubling picture. Newspapers reported on accidents involving Pittsburgh Railways Co. streetcars on an almost daily basis. Not only did passengers suffer injury or death, but pedestrians, horses and wagons and motor vehicles were also frequently involved in collisions with trolleys as they all competed for space on crowded streets. Allegheny County Civil Court indexes at that time also attest to the frequency of accidents as page after page of entries list civil suits people filed against the Pittsburgh Railways Co. Suing the company to recover the cost of medical expenses, lost income or property was a victim's only recourse.

Federal district court records indicate $10 million in accident-related civil claims initially reported to the court in February 1918 had been reduced to $743,378.18 by jury decisions or negotiated settlements by the time the court approved the Pittsburgh Railways Company's bankruptcy discharge petition on December 30, 1925. Three hundred claims, with the earliest dated November 1906, remained unpaid. Fifty-four of the claims were related to the Christmas Eve accident.

Determining how to deal with the unpaid accident claims was a factor the entire time the Pittsburgh Railways Co. remained in receivership. The first formal action occurred on July 7, 1919, when the receivers, Tone, Fagan and George, gained court approval for a policy that would allow them to make settlements when possible for reasonable terms and liquidate or defeat the claims through court proceedings. A second and more significant action came on December 20, 1921, when A.W. Thompson for the Philadelphia Company, J.H. Reid for Pittsburgh Railways and Mayor E.V. Babcock on behalf of the City of Pittsburgh announced the negotiation of the Pittsburgh Agreement, which set the foundation for "adequate street railway service for a reasonable fare," created a Traction Conference Board to provide financial oversight of the transit system for ten years and supported securing a $5 million loan for capital improvements from the Union Trust Company.

Item sixteen of the agreement dealt with the payment of civil claims and stipulated that the reorganized Pittsburgh Railways Co. would pay all judgments and adjust all claims arising from the company's negligent acts prior to April 1918. Assuming that plaintiffs would accept injury and damage awards at face value without interest, the Pittsburgh Railways Co. agreed to making equal, annual installments over a period of ten years, beginning in 1923. The payments would be considered appropriate expenses in the company's annual budget. Pittsburgh City Council approved the agreement in mid-December 1921. It was then submitted to the Pennsylvania Public Services Commission for review, and after a brief delay, commission approval came on February 14, 1922, with the stipulation that the holders of all judgments or claims must agree in writing to the payment terms within thirty days of the commission's approval. The commission also called for the agreement to be implemented by September 1, 1922. On May 18, 1922, the receivers in a court filing confirmed that prior to the Pittsburgh Railways Company's bankruptcy, there were three hundred civil claims representing outstanding obligations of $743,375.18. They also recognized $166,849.66 in claims that had accrued since the receivers took control in 1918. Financial documents at the time also acknowledged personal injury claims amounting to $910,224.81 as current liabilities, "injuries and damages, vehicles and settlements."

On August 27, 1921, Federal District Court judge O.P. Orr appointed former judge Henry G. Wasson as special master to determine whether by reorganizing the Pittsburgh Railways Co. could operate independent of the court's supervision. Wasson, in an opinion issued in March 1923. verified that two-thirds of those holding personal injury and damage judgments had executed written agreements with the Philadelphia Company and the Pittsburgh Railways Co. For the claims that had been taken over or "assigned" by accident victims to various financial institutions in exchange for cash payments, the special master reported that agreements had been reached with the Union Trust Co., Colonial Trust Co. and Guarantee Trust Co. of North America to accept $0.73 on the dollar as the present worth of the claims. The *Pittsburg Press* reported on November 27, 1923, that Wasson had found the Pittsburgh Railways Co. was solvent. The *Gazette Times* later reported that by January 1924, 72 percent of the accident victims representing over $500,000 in claims had agreed to accept face value without interest for their claims.

Although the payment process of civil claims was approved in 1923, the federal district court did not issue an order to initiate payments until March 15, 1924, with the first installment scheduled for early 1926. While no direct or detailed records of the payments exist, the annual reports issued by the Philadelphia Company for the years 1926 to 1935 consistently indicated that Pittsburgh Railways, under the receivers, made all payments as prescribed by the agreement with the City of Pittsburgh. In the report issued in March 1936, the Philadelphia Company acknowledged the final installment had been paid in January 1935, eighteen years after the Knoxville #4236 trolley's Christmas Eve accident.

PITTSBURGH RAILWAYS CO. EXITS RECEIVERSHIP

From 1918 to 1924, the Pittsburgh Railways Co. operated under the court's supervision as a unified street railway system and maintained service to the residents of Pittsburgh and over ninety neighboring municipalities. The system's hundreds of franchise agreements, over 600 miles of track, 69 miles of private rights-of-way, almost 200 bridges and viaducts, 3 inclined planes, 1 tunnel, 33 car barns, 15 power distribution stations, 9 shops, 53 buildings and 1,861 streetcars remained intact. The court-authorized receivership had prevented the underlying companies from breaking their leases with the Pittsburgh Railways Co. and resuming independent operation of the transit companies.

On January 31, 1924, Judge W.H.S. Thompson, at the recommendation of Special Master H. Wasson, rescinded the receivership and returned control of the transit system to its owners. The Union Trust Co. agreed to provide a $5 million loan for capital improvements—$3 million for the purchase of three hundred new streetcars and $2 million for car barns and equipment and to relieve downtown congestion. The reorganization of the transit company began on February 1, 1924.

Twice while under court supervision, Pittsburgh Railways contract disputes with employees ended in strikes. The first walkout, in 1919, lasted two days, until the Federal War Labor Board agreed to increase wages from $0.40 to $0.70 per hour. The projected cost was $1 million for car men and $1 million for other employees. The Pittsburgh Railways Co. wage increase caused concern among transit operators who thought demands for higher wages would ripple across other U.S. cities. A second and seemingly more contentious clash occurred months after the reorganization of the company, in the spring of 1924. A work stoppage by 3,200 motormen and conductors began at midnight on Saturday, May 11, when streetcars were returned to the car barns after contract talks stalled. It was the third strike since 1916. The Pittsburgh Railways Co. responded by bringing in several thousand "auxiliary" or "extraneous" workers from other cities to operate the trollies, which prompted threats of violence in support of the striking workers. The company later announced that it "would not run cars if [the] cars had to storm their way through mobs, and no strongarm tactics would be used under any circumstance." Conductors and motormen then pledged no violence or interference with the extraneous workers.

A front-page *Pittsburg Press* editorial on May 11, 1924, raised concern that temporary workers wouldn't be skilled enough to operate streetcars on

Effects of Street Car Strike–Congestion and Accident.

Upper—Water front along Monongahela river, near Smithfield street bridge, packed with hundreds of automobiles. Lower—Machine wrecked following crash of two cars in Fifth avenue, near Fernando street, yesterday. The accident resulted from congested traffic, it is claimed.

Traffic congestion in downtown Pittsburgh during the Pittsburgh Railways Co. strike in May 1924. *Reprint from* Pittsburgh Post, *May 11, 1924.*

the city's narrow streets, steep grades and dangerous curves. Published concurrent with the editorial was an appeal for public support by the Philadelphia Company president Arthur W. Thompson who stated that motormen and conductors already were paid more than transit workers in any other city or even high school teachers in Pittsburgh. Thompson alleged that increasing wages would keep the company from making capital improvements mandated by the Pittsburgh Agreement.

To ease the strain on the public, the Pittsburgh Railways Co. opened the Mount Washington trolley tunnel, and the city opened the Liberty Tubes to pedestrians on the first day of the strike. Twenty-five walkers were reportedly hospitalized after being overcome by motor vehicle fumes in the Liberty Tunnels. The city also granted emergency permits for store delivery

MEN ARRIVE IN CITY TO REPLACE STRIKERS

Two truck loads, a part of the trainload of 500 men, who arrived in Pittsburgh to replace the striking reet car employes, yesterday.

Pittsburgh Railways Co. recruited motormen and conductors from other cities to work as substitute employees during the strike in May 1924. *Reprint from* Pittsburgh Press, *May 11, 1924.*

trucks, touring cars and carpools to transport people into the city to work and appropriated $25,000 to the police to purchase gas grenades, gas tanks, gas masks and riot guns to ward off protestors.

Violence between the strikes and auxiliary workers was averted when discussions resumed between the Pittsburgh Railways Co. and the union. Pittsburgh mayor William A. Magee played a lead role in bringing the parties back together. Magee believed a protracted strike would end in disaster for the public and would likely force Pittsburgh Railways back into receivership and create the potential for the breakup of the unified system. State and federal mediators, company officials and representatives of the Amalgamated Association of Street and Electric Railway Employees negotiated a two-year agreement with no wage increase and only minor concessions related to the reimbursement for half of the cost of a $28.50 uniform and provision of a better trolley pass ticket for employees.

The three-day strike ended after the workers met at noon and voted 1,071-961 in favor of the proposed contract. The Pittsburgh Railways Co. pledged not to seek a fare increase since the agreement would not result in great additional expense. All strikebreakers were escorted out of the city by police before service resumed. The Knoxville trolley was the first car back in service at 3:44 p.m. on May 13.

Judge Thomson, the following December, discharged the Pittsburgh Railways Co. from court oversight after the receivers filed a final accounting of bankruptcy-related expenses. The company's bankruptcy in 1918 was the first of three experienced by the company between 1918 and 1954. The second occurred in 1938, when Pittsburgh Railways failed to pay interest on outstanding debt following a Depression-generated decline in ridership from 1930 to 1936 and an arbitration award that reduced the workweek for the trolley operators from six to five days without a corresponding reduction in wages.

Between the first and second bankruptcy, discussion about the Pittsburgh Railways Co. in the Philadelphia Company's annual reports suggest that passenger and public safety became a significant focus of attention. In an internal memo recounting "Outstanding Events" for 1928, Pittsburgh Railways general manager W.T. Rossell informed Pittsburgh Railways Co. president A.W. Robertson of the formation of a major accident committee comprised of the heads of various operating departments to investigate and recommend on all accidents of major importance. The annual reports also indicated a steady decline in accidents from 1927 to 1934. In 1927, accidents were reported as 1 per each 3,091 car miles traveled, a 4.2 percent improvement over 1926. The change was attributed to the company's accident prevention policy. No fatalities involving passengers on board the trollies were recorded in 1929. In 1930, accidents involving the public reportedly declined 10.59 percent due to training, supervision and the use of high-grade equipment. In 1931, accidents fell by 14 percent. In 1932, accidents involving the public dropped another 26 percent. An additional 7.59 percent reduction in public accidents occurred in 1934, the year the Pittsburgh Railways Co. received the nationally recognized Andrew N. Brady Safety Award.

The Pittsburgh Railways Co. continued to operate until 1963, when the Port Authority of Allegheny County acquired it and thirty-two other private transit companies to create a countywide public transportation system.

AFTERWORD

Unearthing the details to tell the story of the Mount Washington Tunnel accident has been a rewarding but challenging experience. What started as an attempt to solve a family mystery later turned into a quest to gain a greater understanding of the accident, the victims and its aftermath. Over the years, the reactions of others to this compelling story encouraged me to write for a wider audience. By weaving together evidence gleaned from newspapers, public records and archival materials, my intent was to create an informative account of a tragedy that undoubtedly affected many area families for decades.

My December 31, 2017 article in the *Pittsburgh Post-Gazette* and a presentation made at a local genealogical conference brought reactions I had not expected. People with ties to the story came forward. Their relationships to the accident varied—a victim's granddaughter, a victim's great-nephew and cousin, a family's neighbor and a railroad employee turned rescuer. All added special meaning to my effort. Sharing their messages creates an appropriate closing for this narrative.

As noted earlier, the newspaper accounts of Elmer A. McCoy Jr. and his brother Matthew G. McCoy have stayed with me over the years. Bob McCoy, now a Florida resident, was one of the first people to contact me. His cousin Dave McKeown when reading the *Post Gazette* article had recognized a possible relationship to his McCoy family. Dave's sister, Joy Stascak, sent Bob a link to the article and Bob confirmed that the McCoy boys were their uncles. Bob sent me some news clippings he had found years before

The McCoy children: Elmer Jr., Matthew and Anna. *Courtesy of Bill McKeown.*

at Carnegie Library and reported he had recently arranged for a grave marker at St. Mary's Cemetery in Bloomfield for Elmer and his mother, Anna Gilchrist McCoy. Joy's brother, Bill McKeown, provided the photos of the McCoy children. Anna McCoy was Dave, Joy and Bill's grandmother.

According to Nancy Phillips, Robert and Angela Schmoker Rosenfelter, like many other passengers, were on their way to Christmas shop when they boarded the Knoxville #4236 trolley. Nancy's grandmother Angela Schmoker Rosenfelter lost both her husband, Robert R. Rosenfelter, and an unborn child in the accident. Nancy wrote, "My grandmother survived, she had surgery to have a plate placed in her head to repair her injury, [and] she wore a scar on her forehead for the remainder of her life which was representative of the horror of that day. Angela went on to remarry and had

Top: Robert Rosenfelter, Angela Schmoker's husband. *Courtesy of Barbara and Nancy Phillips.*

Bottom: Angela Schmoker and her brothers, Edward (*left*) and Arthur (*right*). *Courtesy of Barbara and Nancy Phillips.*

seven children, one of which was my mother. One thing that my mother told us long ago is that her mother said that the driver uttered, 'I am taking this trolley to hell' and at the time of the accident thought it meant he was upset about working on Christmas Eve."

Becky Scuillo's story is a curious one. She said that her father, Robert Yonke, and his mother, Gertrude, were friends with a Kestner Family who she believes lived in Mount Oliver. Becky wrote that in 2009, after her grandmother passed away, her father found a box of postcards that for some reason her grandma ended up with but appear to have been Mrs. Bridget (Gorman) Kestner's. The postcards reflect correspondence between members of the Kestner and Gorman families and may or may not have any connection with the Yonke family. Becky wrote, "So, it was coincidental that about the time your article was out, I had read some postcards that were either written by or addressed to Teresa Gorman," a passenger on the Knoxville #4236 trolley who lived at 46 Grape Street, Knoxville. From Becky's information, I was later able to identify that Teresa Gorman was Bridget Kestner's sister.

Sister Marie Grace Blum, OSF, in an e-mail, wrote that my story in the *Pittsburgh Post-Gazette* was a wonderful memoir:

I remember my mother [Grace Kraus Blum] *telling us kids of that accident and how our dad* [William J. Blum] *was one of the men who helped carry the injured into the P&LE office building. My dad was an employee for the railroad and worked in that building in the general manifest office. Our mother would relate that dad's suit was covered with blood and dirt, and a few days or weeks after the terrible happening there were two men who came to our home in Mt. Oliver and offered to have dad's suit cleaned. He declined their offer, saying that that was the least he could do in trying to help the injured people and those who lost their lives. It's no wonder that mother one time told me that she always would pray while riding the street car through that tunnel. I am 85 years old, second youngest of seven children. How I wish that my older siblings were still with us to tell them about this anniversary! I will send the article to my younger sister who may have this memory still....One never knows just how one event may touch in another's history.*

And, in the spring of 2018, I made a presentation about the Knoxville #4236 trolley accident to the South Hills Genealogy Club. I told the story of the Rosenbergers, mother, Christina; daughter, Elfreda; and son, Henry; and used the civil court trial transcript involving Elfreda to demonstrate the ruthlessness of the Pittsburgh Railways Co. in its dealings with accident victims. After the presentation, an attendee, Harold Rosenberger, told me that the Rosenbergers were his twice great-aunt and cousins and confirmed information about the family that I had gleaned from public records. By 1930, Christina and five of her children were living in Florida, where she, Elfreda and another daughter, Johanna, worked as telephone operators in Jacksonville. According to Harold, Elfreda never married, although his grandmother had a picture of her with a boyfriend. Henry "Pitts" Rosenberger worked as a newspaperman in Charleston, West Virginia. Harold Rosenberger recalled that he met Henry once when he was about seventeen or eighteen years old and remembered that he smoked big cigars and liked to drink Scotch.

Each person added to the story of the Mount Washington Tunnel accident. A writer couldn't ask for anything more.

VICTIMS, RESCUERS AND CAREGIVERS

T his listing, compiled from the *Pittsburg Press*, *Pittsburgh Post*, *Pittsburgh Sun*, *Pittsburg Dispatch*, *Pittsburgh Chronicle Telegraph*, *Hilltop Record* and *Gazette Times* from editions published in the days immediately following the Mount Washington Tunnel accident, identifies individuals directly associated with the disaster. In addition to trolley passengers, the motorman and conductor, it includes individuals who sustained injuries when the trolley crashed onto Carson Street, assisted in the rescue of victims or provided medical assistance.

Twenty-three deaths ultimately resulted from the accident: sixteen women and girls and seven men and boys. Allegheny County Coroner's Reports indicate the cause of death for thirteen victims as "entire body was crushed." One of the women was standing on the corner of Carson and Smithfield Streets when she was struck and killed by the trolley. Those who died ranged in age from ten to fifty-seven years; the youngest was Elmer McCoy Jr., the oldest Josephine Retzbach. Of the 112 who were injured, fifty-four were women and girls and fifty-eight were men and boys. Twenty-six of the accident victims immigrated to the Pittsburgh area in the late 1800s and early 1900s.

St. Joseph's Hospital, South Side,
Pittsburg, Pa.

Left: Vintage photo of St. Joseph's Hospital, where many victims were taken after the accident.

Below: Vintage photo of South Side Hospital, another hospital where many victims were treated.

THOSE WHO DIED

Mabel F. Bernett Brecht: age thirty-six, 407 Zara Street, Knoxville. Wife of Martin W. Brecht. Died December 24, 1917, of shock, concussion, compound fractures and lacerations. Buried at South Side Cemetery.

Adele Aglietti Bongiovanni: age forty-two, 404 Charles Street, Knoxville. Wife of Frank Bongiovanni. Died December 26, 1917, at South Side Hospital of pneumonia, a fractured skull and shock. Buried at Calvary Cemetery.

William Randolph Bolitho: age thirty, 141 Charles Street, Knoxville, sheet metal worker. Husband of Amelia B. Williams Bolitho. Died December 24, 1917, of shock and hemorrhage at Mercy Hospital. Buried at South Side Cemetery.

Eugenia Niquet Bricmont: age fifty-seven, 713 Montooth Street, Beltzhoover. Wife of Francis Bricmont. Died December 24, 1917, at accident scene. Buried at St. Joseph's Cemetery.

James Francis Cosgrove: age thirty-nine, 83 West Industry Street, Beltzhoover. Pittsburgh police patrolman. Husband of Catherine M. Dollish Cosgrove. Died December 25, 1917, at St. Joseph's Hospital. Skull fractured and body crushed. Buried at Calvary Cemetery.

Aurelia Kuffner Czerny: age forty-five, 438 Althea Street, Beltzhoover. Wife of Leopold A. Czerny. Died December 24, 1917, at scene of accident. Buried at St. George/St. John Vianney Cemetery.

Pauline Dewmyer: age fifty-three, 600 Fifth Avenue, McKeesport. Clerk. Daughter of Phillip and Catherine Decter Dewmyer. Died December 24, 1917, at accident scene. Buried at Versailles Cemetery.

Caroline M. Fischer: age thirty-nine, 241 Hobart Street, Knoxville. Schoolteacher. Daughter of Jacob and Julia S. Ostermeier Fischer. Died December 24, 1917, at the scene of the accident. Buried at South Side Cemetery.

Howard E. Ford: age twenty-one, 22 Fleet Street, Rankin. Clerk. Son of George E. and Anna May Hurley Ford. Died December 24, 1917, at the accident scene. Buried at Monongahela Cemetery.

Sidney Herbert Frank: age forty-eight, 1922 Fifth Avenue, Altoona. Railroad machinist. Father of Earl, Lillian and William Frank. Died December 24, 1917, in South Side Hospital. Buried at Rose Hill Cemetery, Altoona.

Wesley Jones: age twenty-one, 438 Arabella Street, Knoxville. P&LE Railroad clerk. Son of William R. and Elizabeth Price Jones. Died

December 24, 1917, at St. Joseph's Hospital. Broken left arm, lacerated right hand and internal injuries. Buried in Wilkes-Barre.

Sarah Ethelwyn Kirkham: age twelve, 108 Conniston Avenue, Bon Air. Schoolgirl. Daughter of Walter and Jane Lentz Kirkham. Died December 24, 1917, at scene of accident. Head crushed. Buried at South Side Cemetery.

Mathilda McCabe Klinzing: age thirty-nine, 610 Delmont Street, Beltzhoover. Cashier at Rosenbaum's Market. Wife of Henry Klinzing. Died December 24, 1917, at the scene of accident. Buried in Avaco, Luzerne County. Her stepdaughter, Caroline Klinzing, was also injured.

Elmer A. McCoy Jr.: age ten, 4600 Penn Avenue Rear, Bloomfield. Schoolboy. Son of Elmer A. and Anna Gilchrist McCoy. Died January 8, 1918, at South Side Hospital of meningitis related to a fractured skull. Buried at St. Mary Catholic Cemetery, Lawrenceville. His brother, Matthew McCoy, was injured in the accident.

Clara Miller: age nineteen. Domestic employed by Thomas L. Young, 323 Quincy Avenue, Mount Oliver. Daughter of Joseph and Fannie Hughes Miller. Died on December 24, 1917, at the scene of accident. Buried at Phillipsburg Cemetery, California, PA. Her brother, Frederick H. Miller, was also injured in the accident.

Elizabeth J. Love Patterson: age forty-five, 400 Arabella Street, Knoxville. Wife of Judson A. Patterson. Died December 25, 1917, at St. Joseph's Hospital of shock and fractured skull. Buried at Mount Lebanon Cemetery.

Josephine Rosnagel Retzbach: age sixty-five, 312 South Evaline Street, Bloomfield. Housekeeper for G. Knox and Ethel Barr Chaplin. Widow of John Retzbach. Died December 25, 1917, in St. Joseph's Hospital of a fractured skull and cerebral hemorrhage. Buried at First St. Paul's Evangelical Lutheran Cemetery, Mount Oliver.

Robert R. Rosenfelter: age twenty-six, 126 Arlington Avenue, South Side. Clerk at Atlantic Refining Co. Husband of Angela Schmoker Rosenfelter. Died December 27, 1917, at St. Joseph's Hospital of infection and shock. Buried at Calvary Cemetery.

Clara Belle Delaney Rushway: age twenty-seven, 217 Arabella Street, Knoxville. Wife of Elmer G. Rushway. Died December 24, 1917, at the accident scene. Buried at Calvary Cemetery. Sister of Margaret Miller, who was also injured in the accident.

Ella C. Reardon Sheridan: age fifty-seven, 218 Brownsville Road, Mount Oliver. Wife of Michael A. Sheridan. Died December 24, 1917, at Mercy Hospital of shock, concussion, severe scalp lacerations and compound fractures. Buried at Calvary Cemetery. Her daughter, Gladys, also died as a result of the accident.

Gladys Helen Sheridan: age sixteen, 218 Brownsville Road, Mount Oliver. Student. Daughter of Michael A. and Ella C. Sheridan. Died on January 27, 1918, at St. Joseph's Hospital of septicemia. Buried at Calvary Cemetery.

Clara C. McGrath Tanney: age thirty-one, 209 Jucunda Street, Knoxville. Wife of Joseph A. Tanney. Died December 24, 1917, at the scene of the accident. Buried at Calvary Cemetery. Her brother-in-law, Frank McGeary, was also injured. Her brother, Thomas McGrath, also a trolley passenger, was not injured.

Rose M. Byers Zurlinden: age fifty-six, 604 Lillian Street, Knoxville. Wife of John Zurlinden. Died December 24, 1917, at the scene of the accident. Buried at Homewood Cemetery.

According to the *Pittsburgh Sun*, an unidentified black woman, recorded in newspaper accounts as (no first name) Crawford, age about forty-five, was reportedly crushed when the trolley car overturned onto Carson Street. She sustained head and leg injuries and was taken to Mercy Hospital. The *Gazette Times* stated that Charles Walsh lifted the woman from wreckage and reported that she was so badly injured that she was unrecognizable. Walsh did not think she could survive. She might have been accounted for as the twenty-fourth victim in the Coroner's Jury indictment of the motorman and dispatcher. This woman was never clearly identified in newspaper accounts or public records.

The Injured

Emma Abel: age forty, 409 Jucunda Street, Knoxville. Courthouse matron. Bruised, taken home.

John W. Anthony: age forty-eight, 117 Bausman Street, Knoxville. Principal of Franklin School. Husband of Olive Smith Anthony.

Catherine B. Arthur: age seventeen, South Nineteenth and Sidney Streets, South Side. Daughter of Catherine Flynn and David Arthur. Bruised about head and body. Taken to Mercy Hospital.

Edna Arthur: age thirty-six, 464 Hays Avenue, Mount Oliver (formerly of Indiana, PA). Wife of Harry Arthur. Dislocation of left leg and ankle. Taken to South Side Hospital.

Caroline Young Barrett: age twenty-three, 232 Rochelle Street, Knoxville. Wife of Robert Earl Barrett and daughter of Gustav and Augusta Weyand Young. Barrett later died of complications related to her injuries in November 1919.

Catherine Elizabeth Bauer: age forty-two, 415 Carl Street, Mount Oliver. Wife of George C. Bauer.

Mollie J. Belz: age forty, 45½ Fifteenth Street, Wheeling West Virginia. Bruised about head and body. Taken to Mercy Hospital. Her sister-in-law, Catherine Delaunay, was also injured in the accident.

George Birmingham: age thirty-four, 51 South Fifteenth Street, South Side. Teamster. Left arm and shoulder injured; right leg fractured. Taken to St. Joseph's Hospital.

Mary Borland: age thirty-two South Side. Taken to Allegheny General Hospital.

Mary Bova: age thirty-two, South Side. Wife of Jack Bova.

Frederick John Brown: age twenty-seven, 316 Fifty-Second Street, Lawrenceville. Son of Margaret and Andrew Brown.

Joseph Bruce: age twenty-five, 631 Liberty Avenue, Downtown. Bruised. Taken to St. John's Hospital.

Mary Buba/Bubba: age twenty-three, 129 Rochelle Street, Knoxville. Wife of Frank Bubba.

Viola Butler: age twenty-five, 21 Maine Street, Carrick. Badly lacerated scalp. Taken to South Side Hospital.

Frank Mahard Byers: age twenty-two, 210 Steuben Street, Elliott. Son of William P. and Laura L. Byers.

Mrs. W.J. (Sadie) Byers: age thirty-three, 419 Miller Street, Knoxville. Dislocated right elbow; contusions of head. Taken to South Side Hospital.

H.B. (Hamilton Blaine) Carroll: age thirty-two, 218 Zara Street, Knoxville. Husband of Mayme Armstrong Carroll. Right shoulder and face bruised. Taken home.

Eddie Carter: age eight, 25 Conkling Street, Hill District. Likely son of Edward and Elizabeth Carter.

Beatrice Collingwood: age thirty-four, 138 Zara Street, Knoxville. Wife of Howard J. Collingwood. Contused head; fractured ribs. Taken to South Side Hospital.

Fred Condera (Condello): age twenty-seven, 615 Wylie Avenue, Hill District. Husband of Angeline Condello. Minor injuries. Taken to South Side Hospital.

James Conner: age forty-four, 102 Romeyn Street, Knoxville. Minor injuries. Taken to South Side Hospital.

Harry Coriston: age fourteen, 308 Shaler Street, Mount Washington. Son of John and Louise Gilther Coriston. Bruised head, arms and body. Taken to Mercy Hospital.

Margaret Cox: age forty-three, 399 Bailey Avenue, Mount Washington. Wife of Patrick L. Cox, a yard master for Monongahela Connecting Railroad. Brain injury, lacerations and shock. Taken to South Side Hospital.

Annie Flynn Cready: age forty-six, 106 Amanda Street, Mount Oliver. Wife of John M. Cready. Seriously hurt and unconscious. Taken to Mercy Hospital. Catherine Arthur's aunt.

Leopold Czerny: age forty-eight, 438 Althea Street, Beltzhoover. Husband of Aurelia Kuffner Czerny. Left shoulder and chest injuries, head cut and loss of sight in one eye. Taken to St. Joseph's Hospital.

John S. Davidson: age thirty, 330 Brownsville Road, Knoxville. Husband of Emma Davidson. Head and left shoulder injured and probable internal injuries. Taken to St. Joseph's Hospital.

Mrs. Jules Catherine M. Delaunay: age fifty-three, 5630 Margaretta Street, East Liberty. Wife of prominent merchandise broker, Jules Delaunay. Bad skull wound; bruised about the body. Taken to Mercy Hospital. Sister-in-law of Mollie Belz.

Etra DeMartini: age thirty-three, 306 Bausman Street, Knoxville. Wife of Earnest DeMartini.

Phillip Demme: age fifty-six, 92 Climax Street, Beltzhoover. Husband of Katherine Demme.

Marcella M. Dueck: age fifteen, 63 Amanda Street, Knoxville. Daughter of John and Treasa Brunagle Dueck. Cuts and bruises. Taken home.

Mrs. N.G. (Sadie) Vaux Duvall: age twenty-nine, 229 Rochelle Street, Knoxville. Husband of Nathan G. Duvall. Right shoulder and head bruised. Taken to St. Joseph's Hospital.

Benjamin F. Ellison Jr.: age fifteen, 833 Estella Street, Beltzhoover. Son of Benjamin F. and Emma V. Edwards Ellison.

Mathilda Fischer: age twenty-five, 115 Arlington Avenue, Mount Oliver. Wife of Phillip J. Fischer.

Mrs. Philip C. (Emma Walters) Fischer: age forty-seven, 912 Freeland Street, Knoxville. Minor injuries. Taken to South Side Hospital.

John Flaherty: age twenty-eight, 2013 Larkins Way, South Side. Face and hands cut. Taken to St. Joseph's Hospital.

Nora McDonough Flaherty: age forty, 232 Industry Street, Beltzhoover. Wife of Coleman Flaherty. Lacerations of face and lips. Taken to South Side Hospital.

Stephen James Flaherty: age twenty-two, 3229 Piedmont Street, Dormont. Husband of Maude Cornelius Flaherty.

William Fleming: age twenty-three, 312 Arabella Street, Knoxville. Son of William R. and Violet Jamieson Fleming. Bruised about the head. Taken home.

Charles A. Freeborn: age forty-six, 81 Michigan Street, Beltzhoover. Pittsburgh police detective. Husband of Margaret E. Ronhan Freeborn. Head cut. Taken to St. Joseph's Hospital.

Reverend John P. Gaede: age forty-six, 302 Miller Street, Knoxville, Minister at Seventh-day Adventist church. Husband of Olga Reisenweber Gaede. Dislocated right elbow and shock. Taken to South Side Hospital.

John Gallas: age sixty, 830 Climax Street, Knoxville. Husband of Anna Hombach Gallas. Minor injuries. Taken to South Side Hospital.

Teresa Gorman: age twenty-three, 46 Grape Street, Knoxville. Daughter of Mary and John Gorman. Back and head injuries. Taken to St. Joseph's Hospital.

Thomas H. Hamilton: age forty-one, 7428 Monticello Street, Homewood. Husband of Louisa I. Smith Hamilton. Minor injuries. Taken to South Side Hospital.

Dorothy May Hammett: age fourteen, 332 Orchard Place, Knoxville. Daughter of Wilbert F. and Jessie E. Smith Hammett. Shock. Taken home.

Mrs. W.F. (Wilbert F./Jessie E. Smith) Hammett: age fifty, 332 Orchard Place, Knoxville. Mother of Dorothy May Hammett. Shock. Taken home.

Mrs. F.G. (Minnie) Hanselman: age thirty-six, 609 Gearing Avenue, Knoxville. Wife of Frederick George Hanselman. Face and head cuts and bruises. Taken to St. Joseph's Hospital.

Beatrice Hawk: age fourteen, Zara Street and Virginia Avenue, Knoxville. Daughter of Mary Hawk.

Mary Hawk: age thirty-seven, Zara Street and Virginia Avenue, Knoxville. Contused right shoulder and chest; facial lacerations. Taken to South Side Hospital.

Irene Herrington: age eighteen, 402 Knox Avenue, Knoxville. Daughter of Fred and Alice Whitely Herrington. Cut and bruised about face and body.

John T. Herrington: age twenty-three, 944 Brownsville Road, Mount Oliver. Husband of Ella L. Herrington. Likely Mrs. Charles (Jennie) Reilly's brother.

Mrs. Stanistawa Jiackowski: age twenty-one, 2512 Josephine Street, South Side. Wife of Wladyslaw S. Jiackowski. Taken to Allegheny General Hospital.

Martin Joyce: age twenty-two, 119 Cagwin Street, Beechview. Son of John M. and Bridget Keane Joyce.

Morris Julius: age twenty-one, 1840 Bedford Avenue, Hill District. Son of Abraham and Blanche Julius. Right leg injured; body bruised. Taken home.

Thomas (Tomys) Kahnych: age thirty-six, 326 Olivia Street, McKees Rocks. Husband of Sophia Kahnych.

Mrs. Henry Kalkos: age forty, 133 Stamm Avenue, Mount Oliver. Fractured left ankle; injured right shoulder. Taken to South Side Hospital.

Herman H. Klingler: age twenty-five, 16 Penelope Street, Mount Washington. Son of George E. Sr. and Elizabeth Erk Klingler, Library (South Park). Taken to South Side Hospital.

Caroline Klinzing: age twenty, 610 Delmont Street, Beltzhoover. Daughter of Henry and Mathilda McCabe Klinzing.

Whitney Stephenson Knight: age twelve, 98 Ridgewood Street, West View. Son of George J. and Gertrude H. Kearns Knight. Bruised face and body. Taken to St. Joseph's Hospital for treatment.

Thomas Kinlock: age twelve, 123 Front Street, Brownsville. Son of Iva Donaldson and George Kinlock, Minor injuries. Taken to South Side Hospital.

Dorothy Devine Lafferty: age nineteen, 203 Kingsboro Street, Allentown. Wife of Clifford Bruce Lafferty.

Tillie Caroline Lauer: age thirty-eight, 15 Willis Street, Carrick. Daughter of Gustave and Catherine Keck Lauer of Jefferson, Butler County. Head and left arm injured. Taken to St. Joseph's Hospital.

James Leonard: age thirty-nine, 518 South Craig Street, Oakland. Husband of Edith E. Williams Leonard. Trampled, bruised about head and nose broken. Taken to Mercy Hospital and then home.

Charles J. Langhurst: age thirty-three, 73 McLain Avenue, Allentown. Husband of Florence E. Williams Langhurst. Minor injuries. Taken to South Side Hospital.

Robert "Bobbie" Mallory: age thirteen, 17 Fernando Street, Hill District. Son of Nell Mallory. Head lacerations and left wrist broken. Taken to South Side Hospital.

John Henry Martin: age fifty-two, 240 Charles Street, Knoxville. Husband of Alma Chester Martin. Minor injuries. Treated at South Side Hospital.

George McBee: age thirteen, 290 Ottawa Street, Mount Washington. Scalp wounds and bruised body. Treated at Mercy Hospital.

J.F. (James Federick) McCann: age forty-three, 371 Grace Street, Youngstown, Ohio.

Matthew G. McCoy: age eight, 4600 Penn Avenue Rear, Bloomfield. Son of Elmer and Anna McCoy. Facial cuts. Taken home.

Frank (Francis) R. McGeary: age twenty-three, 805 Tobin Street, North Side. Son of Bridget Moran and the late Patrick McGeary. Brother-in-law of Clara Tanney.

Thomas F. McGrath: age nineteen, 150 Warrington Avenue, Beltzhoover. Son of Thomas F. and Catherine Fleckenstein McGrath. Head and arm cuts. Taken to St. Joseph's Hospital.

Bernard J. McKenna: age thirty-eight, hotel keeper, 2107 Penn Avenue, Strip District. Skull fractured; unconscious. Taken home after treated at hospital.

B.C. (Bernard Campbell) McMeal: age fifty-eight, 316 Meridian Street, Mount Washington. P&LE Railroad employee. Husband of Elizabeth Corbett McMeal. Injured when he helped rescue accident victims. Head injury, treated at scene, then take home.

Howard B. McNutt: age thirty-eight, 430 Rochelle Street, Knoxville. PA Tube Co. official. Husband of Bertha J. Whitten McNutt. Father of John McNutt, who was also injured in the accident. Fractured left ankle, scalp wounds and fractured ribs. Taken to South Side Hospital.

John McNutt: age twelve, 430 Rochelle Street, Knoxville. Son of Howard B. and Bertha J. McNutt. Broken left leg; fractured left arm. Taken to South Side Hospital.

Alicia (Hyland) Mercer: age twenty-nine, 315 Beltzhoover Avenue, Beltzhoover. Wife of Albert G. Mercer.

Jennie S. Mercer: age sixty-three, 315 Beltzhoover Avenue, Beltzhoover. Widow of George F. Mercer.

Mary M. Merkle: age about fifty-two, 236 Hays Street, Mount Oliver. Minor injuries. Treated at South Side Hospital.

Alexander V. Miller: age thirty-five, 422 Hays Avenue, Mount Oliver. Husband of Estella M. Langersfeld Miller. Head and left arm injured, five ribs fractured, probable internal injuries. Taken to St. Joseph's Hospital.

Mrs. Albert A. (Margaret Delaney) Miller: age twenty-seven, 233 Arabella Street, Knoxville. Daughter of Frank and Jennie Shea Delaney. Clara Rushway's sister. Head and left arm cut; body bruised. Taken to St. Joseph's Hospital.

Frederick (Fred) Hughes Miller: age twenty, 208 Cable Avenue, East Pittsburgh. Brother of Clara Miller. Facial cuts, three ribs fractured. Taken to St. Joseph's Hospital.

Alma Morris: age thirty-nine, 449 Michigan Street, Beltzhoover. Contused back and shoulder, shock. Taken to St. Joseph's Hospital.

Charles Newman: age thirty-two, 517 Delmont Street, Beltzhoover. Son of John J. and Henrietta Newman/Neuman.

Laura Nestor: age thirty, 859 Ashdale Street, Beltzhoover. Wife of Patrick Nestor.

Mrs. Edward J. (Laura M. Alexander) Ohl: age thirty-eight, 212 Summit Street, Knoxville. Left arm fractured, head cut and unconscious. Taken to St. Joseph's Hospital.

John P. O'Malley: age twenty-four, 235 Zara Street, Knoxville. *Pittsburgh Post* stereographer. Son of John R. and Annie Bradley O'Malley. Cut forehead and bruised leg.

Anna Patterson: age forty-three, 615 Estella Street, Beltzhoover. Head and facial cuts. Taken to St. Joseph's Hospital.

William H. Pickles: age forty-five, 115 Olcott Street, Crafton. Husband of Margaret Jones Pickles. Serious head injuries and two broken legs. Taken to Mercy Hospital.

Robert C. Quinn: age twenty-seven, 414 Charles Street, Knoxville. Husband of Sarah E. Vernon Quinn.

Mrs. Charles (Jennie Herrington) Reilly: age thirty-seven, 728 Lillian Street, Knoxville. Cut and bruised face and body. Taken to St. Joseph's Hospital.

Charles A. Roberts: age thirty-four, 434 Ruxton Avenue, Mount Washington, P&LE Railroad conductor. Husband of Ella Stewart Roberts. Back sprain and kidney injuries. Taken to South Side Hospital.

Frank Rodgers: age twenty-seven, 52 Southern Avenue, Mount Washington. P&LE accountant. Husband of Gladys Uhlam Rodgers. Aided in rescue of victims.

Christina Rosenberger: age thirty-six, 327 Hobart Street, Knoxville. Widow of Carl Rosenberger. Mother of Elfreda and Henry Rosenberger. Left arm injured. Taken to St. Joseph's Hospital.

Elfreda (Freda) Rosenberger: age twenty-two, 327 Hobart Street, Knoxville. Telephone operator. Head crushed, face severely cut, internal injuries. Unconscious when taken to St. Joseph's Hospital.

Henry Rosenberger: age thirteen, 327 Hobart Street, Knoxville. Student.

Angela Schmoker Rosenfelter: age twenty-five, 120 Arlington Avenue, South Side. Wife of Robert R. Rosenfelter. Head injury, probably internal injuries. Taken to St. Joseph's Hospital.

Henrietta E.A. Schlegel: age fifty-nine, 73 Harwood Street, Mount Washington. Widow of Charles A. Schlegel. Mother-in-law of Mrs. W.W. Schlegel.

Mrs. W.W. (Lydie Casey Stewart) Schlegel: age thirty-one, 73 Harwood Street, Mount Washington. Wife of Walter W. Schlegel. Minor injuries. Treated at South Side Hospital.

Conrad Scherer: age twenty-six, 256 Arlington Avenue, Allentown. Son of John and Catherine Scherer. Minor injuries. Treated at South Side Hospital.

Walter Schorr: age forty-five, 2310 Milligan Avenue, Swissvale. Husband of Edna M. Ryan Schorr. Right shoulder and head bruised. Taken to St. Joseph's Hospital.

August Schorr: age forty-six, 2238 Milligan Avenue, Swissvale. Husband of Elizabeth M. Kraus.

Frances Johanna Schulze: age forty-five, 500 Gearing Avenue, Beltzhoover. Wife of Harry Schulze. Treated for shock and taken home.

Nelson Vance Shook: age twenty-eight, 1920 Library Road, Castle Shannon. Husband of Irene Handel Shook. Nose fractured, cuts on face and body. Taken to St. Joseph's Hospital.

Nellie (Winters) Simmons: age thirty, 502 Chalfont Street, Beltzhoover. Wife of Walter D. Simmons. Cut and bruised face and body. Taken to St. Joseph's Hospital.

William R. Simpson: age fourteen, 60 Lafferty Avenue, Beltzhoover. Son of James and Frances E. Simpson. Head bruised. Taken to St. Joseph's Hospital.

C.L.H. Smith: age fifty-two, 110 Fourth Street, Wheeling, West Virginia. Husband of Elizabeth Smith.

Reverend George T. Smith: age fifty, 28 Lafferty Avenue, Beltzhoover. Pastor of St. Paul's AME Church and field secretary of Wilbur Force

University. Husband of Anne R. Anderson Smith. Bruised head and arms. Taken to Mercy Hospital.

Mrs. John W. (Blanche Parker) Thompson: age nineteen, Zelienople. Daughter of Frank L. and Julia B. Craighead Parker.

Fred B. Vondera: age thirty-six, 218 Penn Avenue, Mount Oliver. Right arm and leg contused, sprained back. Taken to South Side Hospital.

Howard Young: age nine, 223 Beltzhoover Avenue, Beltzhoover. Son of Howard S. and Gertrude W. Brandt Young. Slight facial injuries. Taken home after treatment at St. Joseph's Hospital.

Kate McMahon Young: age sixty-five, 622 Climax Street, Beltzhoover. Widow of Peter Young.

Allegheny County Coroner's Office official documents recorded the names of individuals who worked with the coroner as deputies and doctors and nursing supervisors who worked at the hospitals and cared for the accident victims.

CAREGIVERS

Deputy Coroners: Hugh M. Gilmore (167 Manton Way, Allentown); Joseph R. Borland (6102 Broad Street, Friendship); Hugh D. Dempsey (1913 Forbes Avenue, The Bluff); Anthony Schaefer (2220 Jane Street, South Side); Harry T. Ewing (3810 Fifth Avenue, Oakland); Samuel Shenkan (73 Congress Street, Downtown Pittsburgh); Michael J. Horan (714 Wharton Street, South Side); George Liffert (46 South Eleventh Street, South Side); John D. McKinley (519 Ringold Street, McKeeport); John Danner (433 North Graham Street, Garfield); and Thomas J. O'Brien (1431 Boyle Street, North Side)

Mercy Hospital: John H. Seipel, MD (2535 Forbes Avenue, Oakland)

St. Joseph's Hospital: Sr. M. Bonaventure, superintendent (resided at the hospital); Lawrence E. Rectenwald, MD (1820 Ley Avenue, Troy Hill); and Thaddeus J. Telerski, MD (St. Francis Hospital, Forty-Fifth Street, Lawrenceville)

South Side Hospital: Jeannette L. Jones, superintendent (resided at the hospital); A.A. Biddle, MD (no local address found); Charles C. Lang, MD (504 Brookline Boulevard, Brookline); and F.L. Thigpen, MD (no local address found)

REFERENCES

Introduction

"The Growth of Pittsburgh—Annexation and Population." Brookline Connection. http://www.brooklineconnection.com/history/Facts/Growth.html.

Hobbs, Frank, and Nicole Stoops. "Demographic Trends in the 20th Century." U.S. Census Bureau Census 2000 Special Reports, Series CENSR-4. Washington, D.C.: U.S. Government Printing Office, 2002.

Knoxville Borough: A History. Knoxville, PA: Pittsburgh Women's Library of Pittsburgh, 1938.

Lorant, Stefan. *Pittsburgh*. 5th ed. Pittsburgh, PA: Esselmont Books, 1999.

Miller, Edward J., and Joel A. Tarr. *Making Industrial Pittsburgh Modern*. Pittsburgh, PA: University of Pittsburgh Press, 2019.

Murdock, Frank R. "Some Aspects of Pittsburgh's Industrial Contribution to the World War." *Western Pennsylvania Historical Magazine* 4 (October 1921): 214–23.

Penna, Anthony N. "Changing Images of Twentieth Century Pittsburgh." *Pennsylvania History: A Journal of Mid-Atlantic Studies* 43(January 1976): 48-63.

Pittsburgh Board of Public Education. *Course of Study in Geographic, Biographic and Historic Pittsburgh*. Teacher's manual. Pittsburgh, PA: Board of Public Education, 1921.

Pittsburgh Post. "Local Draft Boards on New Work Today." December 12, 1917.

Pittsburg Press. "Enraged City to Wage Fight Against Trolley Fare Increase." December 22, 1917.

———. "Pittsburgh Is Clad in Khaki This Season." December 24, 1917.

———. "State Gets 1,550,000 Red Cross Members." January 26, 1918.

Pittsburgh (PA) Transit Commissioner. "Report of Transit Commissioner to the Honorable Mayor and the City Council of the City of Pittsburgh." Pittsburgh, PA: Transit Commissioner, 1917.

U.S. Department of Commerce, Bureau of the Census. *Fourteenth Census of the United States, State Compendium—Pennsylvania*. Washington, D.C.: Government Printing Office, 1924.

———. *Thirteenth Census of the United States, State Compendium—Pennsylvania*. Washington, D.C.: Government Printing Office, 1912.

———. *Twelfth Census of the United States, State Compendium—Pennsylvania*. Washington, D.C.: Government Printing Office, 1901.

———. *Union Scale of Wages and Hours of Labor, May 15, 1919: Bulletin of the United States Bureau of Labor Statistics, No. 274*. Washington, D.C.: Government Printing Office, September 1920. http//:fraser.stlouisfed.org/.../union-scale-wages- hours-labor-may-15-1919-476872.

———. *Union Scale of Wages and Hours of Labor, May 15, 1917: Bulletin of the United States Bureau of Labor Statistics, No. 245*. Washington, D.C.: Government Printing Office, March 1919. http//:fraser.stlouisfed.org/.../union-scale-wages-hours-labor-may-15-1917-476870.

U.S. Treasury Department, Office of Commissioner of Internal Revenue. *Statistics of Income*. Washington, D.C.: Government Printing Office, 1916–37. https://www.irs.gov/statistics/soi-tax-stats-historical-data-tables.

Chapter 1

"Damage of One Stick of Dynamite." DSL Reports. https://www.dslreports.com/forum/r21659321-Damager-of-one-stick-of-dynamite.

Gazette Times. "Christmas Shoppers Victims of Capsized Knoxville Streetcar." December 25, 1917.

———. "Hundreds Hurried to the Morgue and Hospitals to See Victims." December 25, 1917.

———. "Tunnel Stop Denied by Motorman, but Affirmed by Others." December 26, 1917.

———. "250,000 Join Red Cross in Big Drive Here." December 25, 1917.

Kuffner, Alan P., ME. Consultation with author on calculation and interpretation of trolley crash impact, May 2019 and May 2020.

Pittsburgh Dispatch. "Children Trampled in Midst of Ruins." December 25, 1917.

———. "18 Killed, 82 Injured When Car Is Torn to Pieces at Tunnel." December 25, 1917.

Pittsburgh Post. "Passengers on Runaway Car Caught Crash Struggle for Release." December 25, 1917.

———. "Soldier Beats Man Robbing Car Victims." December 25, 1917.

———. "Statement Issued by Coroner Jamison." December 2v5, 1917.

———. "Wreck Survivors Tell of Awaiting Fate in Car Crash." December 25, 1917.

Pittsburg Press. "Crew of Wrecked Car Clashed, Say Women Passengers." December 26, 1917.

Pittsburgh Sun. "36 People Still in Hospital; Four Likely to Die." December 26, 1917.

Chapter 2

Evening News (Wilkes-Barre, PA). "Westmore Man Meets Death in Pittsburgh." December 26, 1917.

Gazette Times. "Boy Hurt in Knoxville Car Disaster Dies in Hospital." January 1, 1918.

———. "City Detective Painfully Injured, Does Rescue Work." December 25, 1917.

———. "Daddy Is Lisp of Lad Dying in Hospital." December 26, 1917.

———. "Engaged Couple Killed on Way to Purchase Present." December 25, 1917.

———. "James Cosgrove." December 27, 1917.

———. "Knoxville Man Is Fatally Injured in Trolley Accident." December 25, 1917.

———. "Knoxville Woman in Wreck Loses Money and Jewelry." December 25, 1917.

———. "Mother of Dead Girl Had Premonition of Child's Fate." December 25, 1917.

———. "Motorman H.H. Klingler Charged with Manslaughter." December 27, 1917.

———. "Sad Holiday for Many in South Hills." December 25, 1917.

———. "Soldier's Death Denied Boy; Crushed in Trolley Tragedy." December 26, 1917.

———. "Teacher Leaves Her Sickbed and Is Killed in Car Accident." December 25, 1917.

———. "Wreck Tragedy Enters Many Homes in City." December 25, 1917.

Hilltop Record. "Accident's Shadow Hits Eistefford." December 28, 1917.

———. "Lights and Shadows of Disaster." December 28, 1917.

Pittsburgh Chronicle Telegraph. "Fatal Car Wreck Brings Woe and Misery to Many." December 25, 1917.

Pittsburgh Dispatch. "Bleeding from Torn Head, Woman Unnoticed by Crowd." December 25, 1917.

———. "Children Trampled in Midst of Ruins." December 25, 1917.

———. "18 Killed, 82 Injured When Car Is Torn to Pieces at Tunnel." December 25, 1917.

———. "Mother's Fears Realized When Father Finds Girl at Morgue." December 25, 1917.

———. "Wreck Due to Crowded Cars, Declares Girl Who Escaped." December 25, 1917.

Pittsburgh Post. "Black Cloud of Tragedy Darkens Christmas Day in Homes of Knoxville." December 26, 1917.

———. "Boy, Hurt in Wreck; Going to Buy Gifts." December 25, 1917.

———. "Frantic Crowds Besiege Morgue and Hospitals." December 25, 1917.

———. "The Holiday Tragedy." Editorial, December 28, 1917.

———. "Wreck Survivors Tell of Awaiting Fate in Car Crash." December 25, 1917.

Chapter 3

Gazette Times. "Angry Crowd Stones Car and Injures Woman." December 26, 1917.

———. "Car Service Complaints Heard Today." January 17, 1918.

———. "Confiscation of Street Car Property, Threat of Knoxville." December 27, 1917.

———. "Coroner Deplores Increase in Deaths by Violence Here." January 4, 1918.

———. "Council Plans to Arrest Crews When Cars Are Congested." December 27, 1917.

———. "Higher Fares Start, Court Denies Pleas." January 22, 1918.

———. "Knoxville for Safety." January 3, 1918.

———. "Operation of Cars through Tunnel Is Criticized." December 25, 1917.

———. "Public Service Body Sought as Trolley Car Dictator Here." December 27, 1917.

———. "Radical Remedies Are Advocated for Traction Co." January 4, 1918.

———. "South Hills May Unite to Fight Pittsburgh." December 30, 1917.

———. "Trolley Probe by Knoxville Investigators." December 29, 1917.

———. "Tunnel Wreck Soon May Go to Grand Jury." December 28, 1917.

Hilltop Record. "Brentwood Solons Extend Sympathy to Stricken Boro." December 28, 1917.

———. "Carrick Council Voices Sympathy." January 4, 1918.

———. "High Spots in Car Situation in Pittsburgh." December 28, 1917.

———. "Mass Meeting Urges Haddock to Prevent Possible Rioting." January 11, 1918.

———. "Possibility of Rioting Is Seen as Fare Raise Date Approaches." January 11, 1918.

"Indignation." Definition adapted from the *Cambridge Advanced Learner's Dictionary & Thesaurus*. New York: Cambridge University Press, 2018. https://dictionary.cambridge.org/ dictionary/english/indignation.

Pittsburgh Chronicle Telegraph. "Another Crowded Car Jumps Track." December 27, 1917.

———. "Homeville Maids Cause Conductor to Run to Safety." January 16, 1918.

———. "Hundreds Walk Through Tunnel." January 15, 1918.

———. "Lives Endangered When Knoxville Car Runs Away." January 11, 1918.

Pittsburgh Post. "Cars 'Kidnapped' by Angry Crowds." January 12, 1918.

———. December 28, 1917.

———. January 4, 1918.

———. "Knoxville Car Runs Wild Down Grade." January 12, 1918.

———. "3177 Deaths Is County's 1913 Record." January 1, 1914.

Pittsburg Press. "Coroner Jamison in Report Deplores Lack of Safety Here., January 4, 1917.

———. "Death Toll in Tragedy Soars to 20." December 26, 1917.

———. "Industries Hit by Poor Car Service; South Hills Protest." January 11, 1918.

———. "Lack of Care Causes Wreck; Says Prober." January 17, 1918.

———. "Mayor Names a Car Service Body." January 22, 1918.

———. "100 Men Trudge through Tunnel; Trolleys Tied Up." January 15, 1918.

———. "Panic Ensues When Knoxville Car Runs Wild; Brakes Fail." January 11, 1918.

———. "Plan to Arrest Officials of Railways Company." December 27, 1917.

———. "Three Big Cars in Smash." January 27, 1918.

———. "Thirteen Hurt in Wreck." January 16, 1905.

———. "$2,095,000 in Carfares Paid as Rental to Old Companies." January 17, 1918.

Pittsburgh Sun. "Knoxville Car Runs Wild on Steep Grade." January 12, 1918.

———. "Knoxville Secret Service Men Busy." December 27, 1917.

Chapter 4

Gazette Times. "Christmas Tree Standing." December 26, 1917.

Hartford, Margaret E. *Allegheny County's Americans by Choice*. Pittsburgh, PA: American Service Institute of Allegheny County, 1944, 17.

Madarasz, Anne. *Glass Shattering Notions*. Pittsburgh, PA: Historical Society of Western Pennsylvania, 1998.

Naturalization Petitions of the U.S. District Court, 1820–1930, and Circuit Court, 1820–1911, for the Western District of Pennsylvania. NAI Number 173. Record Group Title *M1537*. National Archives, Washington, D.C.

Pittsburgh Post. "Frantic Crowds Besiege Morgue and Hospitals, Boy Identifies Mother." December 24, 1917.

———. "Tree Was Trimmed." December 26, 1917.

Chapter 5

Booth & Flinn Company. *70 Years of General Contracting: A Review of Major Construction Accomplishments of Booth & Flinn Company, General Contractors, Pittsburgh, Pa. 1876–1946*. Pittsburgh, PA: privately published, 1946.

Canonsburg (PA) Notes, September 27, 1901.

City of Pittsburgh Department of Planning. S.L. Boggs Plan, Plan No. 2 Plan Book, Vol. 9, 44–45.

"Designing American Lenticular Truss Bridges 1878–1900." History Cooperative. https://historycooperative.org/journal/designing-american-lenticular-truss-bridges-1878-1900/.

Parkinson, Tom E. *The Street Railways of Pittsburgh, 1859–1967*. Pittsburgh: Light Railway Transport League and the Pennsylvania Railway Museum Association, 1973.

Pittsburg Dispatch, December 1, 1904.

Pittsburgh Gazette, June 21, 1902; June 26, 1902; October 7, 1904 and December 1, 1904.

Pittsburgh Post, February 2, 1902; March 19, 1902; June 5, 1903; October 7, 1904 and December 2, 1904.

Pittsburg Press, February 2, 1902; March 11, 1902; March 15, 1902; April 22, 1902; April 25, 1902; May 9, 1902; June 3, 1902; June 5, 1902; June 6, 1907; June 17, 1902; June 20, 1902; June 22, 1902; June 25, 1902; June 30, 1902; July 13, 1902; September 1, 1902; September 9, 1902; September 26, 1902; October 8, 1902; January 17, 1903; April 14, 1903; April 16, 1903; June 22, 1903; October 6, 1903; June 9, 1904; June 2, 1905; July 15, 1904; November 12, 1904; November 17, 1904 and December 1, 1904.

Pittsburgh Railways Company Records, 1872–1974, AIS.1974.29. Archives and Special Collections, University of Pittsburgh Library System Series I. Snow Report, 1872–1917.

Pittsburgh Transit Commissioner. *Report of Transit Commissioner to the Honorable Mayor and the City Council of the City of Pittsburgh*. Pittsburgh, PA: Transit Commissioner, 1917.

Port Authority of Allegheny County, Pennsylvania. "As Built Plans." South PATWAY, August 31, 1971, and "As Built Plans." South PATWAY, August 20, 1975.

Van Trump, James V. *Station Square: A Golden Age Revived*. Pittsburgh, PA: Pittsburgh History & Landmarks Foundation, 1978.

Chapter 6

Fleming, George T. *History of Pittsburgh & Environs: From Prehistoric Days to the Beginning of the American Revolution*. Vol. 2. New York: American Historical Society, 1922.

Lind, Alan R. *From Horsecars to Streamliners: An Illustrated History of the St. Louis Car Company*. Park Forest, IL: Transport History Press, 1978.

Miller Library. Pennsylvania Trolley Museum. Washington. PA.

Pittsburgh Transit Commissioner. Report of Transit Commissioner to the Honorable Mayor and the City Council of the City of Pittsburgh. Pittsburgh, PA: Transit Commissioner, 1917.

St. Louis Car Company Records (Pittsburgh Railways Order 996, 1914). Department of Special Collections, Washington University Libraries.

Young, Andrew D. *The St. Louis Car Company Album.* Glendale, CA: Interurban Press, 1984.

Young, Andrew D., and Eugene F. Provenzo. *The History of the St. Louis Car Company "Quality Shops."* San Diego, CA: Howell-North Books, 1978.

Chapter 7

Allegheny County Coroner's Office Records, 1884–1976, AIS 1982.07. Archives and Special Collections, University of Pittsburgh Library System. Series I. Coroner's Case File 191802, 203–228.

Gazette Times. "Coroner Jamison to Make Rigid Investigation." December 25, 1817.

———. "Dohoney to Investigate Pittsburgh Car Disaster." December 25, 1917.

———. "Jury to Sit at Inquest." December 29, 1917.

———. "Klingler Held in Jail, Says He Was Sober." December 30, 1917.

———. "Knoxville Car Brakes Safe, Says Report." January 17, 1918.

———. "Motorman Charged with Manslaughter." December 27, 1917.

———. "Tunnel Stop Denied by Motorman, but Affirmed by Others." December 26, 1917.

———. "Tunnel Wreck Probe Soon May Go to Grand Jury." December 28, 1917.

Hilltop Record. "Dispatcher and Klingler to Grand Jury." February 22, 1918.

———. "Traction Tragedy Laid to Crowding." December 28, 1917.

Pittsburgh Chronicle Telegraph. "Businessmen to Be Coroner's Jury in Wreck Probe." December 28, 1917.

———. "Dohoney to Investigate Pittsburgh Car Disaster." December 26, 1917.

———. "Motorman May Be Indicted." December 27, 1917.

———. "Motorman Seems as One in Dream When Put in Jail." December 29, 1917.

———. "Mrs. Bongiovanni Twentieth Victim of Trolley Crash." December 26, 1917.

———. "Railway Company Is Advised to Stop Overloading Cars." February 21, 1918.

Pittsburgh Dispatch. "State Demands Data on Fatal Car Wreck, Motorman Arrested." December 27, 1917.

———. "Twin Probe Planned in Car Wreck." December 29, 1917.

Pittsburgh Post. "Blame Fixed by Coroner's Jury." February 21, 1918.

———. "Jamison Ends Investigation of Car Wreck." December 25, 1917.

———. "Overcrowding Caused Wreck Says Dohoney." December 25, 1917.

Pittsburg Press. "Coroner Has Klingler Virtually Under Arrest at South Side Hospital." December 26, 1917.

———. "Crowds Attend Fatal Wreck Inquisition." February 20, 1918.

———. "Death Toll in Tragedy Soars to 20—Motorman Quizzed by the Authorities." December 26, 1917.

Pittsburgh Sun. "Coroner Is Prepared to Hold Car Inquest." December 26, 1917.

———. "Jury Considers Verdict on Car Disaster." February 20, 1918.

———. "Motorman of Death Car Changes Story." December 26, 1917.

———. "Motorman of Death Car Is Held at Jail." December 26, 1917.

———. "Overcrowding Caused Wreck Says Dohoney." December 29, 1917.

Chapter 8

Allegheny County Department of Court Records, Civil/Family Division. Adsectum Index to Appearance Docket Court of Common Pleas, July Term 1916–April 1918.

———. Adsectum Index to Appearance Docket Court of Common Pleas, July Term 1918–April 1920.

———. Elfreda Rosenberger v. Pittsburgh Railways Company, No. 47 July Term 1918. C.P. Allegheny County. (Trial transcript.)

Allegheny County Department of Court Records, Criminal Division. Coroner's Inquest, Vol. 124. March 18 and 19, 1918, 204. *Clara Tanney et. al. v. Herman Henry Klingler.*

Allegheny County Department of Court Records, Criminal Division. Court of the Oyer and Terminer and General Jail Delivery. *Commonwealth v. Herman Henry Klingler* March Session 1918. (Various documents related to Grand Jury indictment of H.H. Klingler and M.F. Maley on twenty-three counts of involuntary manslaughter; trial of H.H. Klingler and conviction on two counts related to Clara Tanney and Ella Sheridan; Attorney William Brennen's petitions on behalf of H.H. Klingler regarding charge to jury and double jeopardy; District Attorney Harry H. Rowand's petition to try H.H. Klingler for twenty additional charges; judge's instruction to jury and jury's subsequent decision to drop twenty involuntary manslaughter charges; and finding of insufficient evidence to prosecute Pittsburgh Railways dispatcher, M.F. Maley.)

Coroner's Case File 194701-235 Hamilton B. Carroll Allegheny County. Coroner's Office Records, 1884–1976, AIS.1982.07. Archives and Special Collections, University of Pittsburgh Library System. Subseries 1. Coroner Case Files 1887–1973.

Daily Republican (Monongahela PA). "Indicted for Involuntary Manslaughter." March 14, 1918.

———. "Klingler No Further Prosecution." September 21, 1920.

Gazette Times. "Jury Convicts Motorman in Tunnel Crash." February 14, 1919.

———. "Liquor Figured in Car Wreck Testimony." February 12, 1919.

———. "Tunnel Death Car Motorman Put on Trial." February 11, 1919.

———. "Tunnel Indictments Dropped." September 21, 1920.

Pennsylvania Superior Court. Christina Rosenberger and Henry Rosenberger, her son v. Pittsburgh Railways Co. Motion for New Trial. No. 48 July Term, 1918. C.P. Allegheny County.

Pittsburgh Post. "Jury Convicts Klingler on Two Charges as Result of Tunnel Wreck." February 14, 1919.

———. "Klingler Case Evidence in Hands of Jury." February 13, 1919.

———. "Klingler Held by Grand Jury for 23 Deaths." March 14, 1918.

———. "State to End Case Against Motorman in Tunnel Wreck Trial Today." February 13, 1919.

———. "Three Score Challenged to Set Jury in Fatal Tunnel Wreck Trial." February. 11, 1919.

Pittsburgh Post-Gazette "River Victim Is Beaver Man." January 15, 1947.

Pittsburg Press. "Asks New Trial for 'Death Car' Motorman." February 18, 1919.

———. "Body in River Identified as Ex-Beaver Fireman." January 15, 1947.

———. "Convict Klingler on Two Counts." February 13, 1919.

———. "Death Car Driver Faces 20 Charges." September 19, 1920.

———. "Klingler Faces 20 More Death Charges." September 18, 1920.

———. "Klingler Faces Indictments in 23 Cases Where Victims Died after Big Wreck." February 10, 1919.

———. "Motorman Gets Fifteen Months in Penitentiary." July 10, 1919.

———. "State Rests in Prosecution of Klingler; Jury Hears Address." February 12, 1919.

———. "Tunnel Death Car Conductor Aids Defense by Reversing Inquest Story." February 11, 1919.

Chapter 9

Allegheny County Bar Association. "Bolitho v. Pittsburgh Railways Co. Motion for New Trial. No. 2228 July Term, 1918." *Pittsburgh Legal Journal* 69 (1919): 327.
———. "Christina Rosenberger and Elfreda Rosenberger, Her Daughter v. Pittsburgh Railways Co. Motion for New Trial. No. 47 July Term, 1918." *Pittsburgh Legal Journal* 68 (1920): 459–60.
———. "Christina Rosenberger v. Pittsburgh Railways Co. Motion for New Trial. No. 49 July Term 1918." *Pittsburgh Legal Journal* 68 (1920): 448.
———. "Miller v. Pittsburgh Railways Co. Motion for New Trial. No. 1405, July Term 1918." *Pittsburgh Legal Journal* 69 (1921): 30–32.
Pre-Receivership Judgments, Personal Injury and Damage, as of March 22, 1922. U.S. District Court, Western District of Pennsylvania, Equity Case File No. 201, May Term 1918. "American Brake Shoe and Foundry Co. et al v. Pittsburgh Railway Co." National Archives and Records Administration, Kansas City MO.

Chapter 10

Agreement between City of Pittsburgh, Philadelphia Company and Pittsburgh Railways Company, December 20, 1921.
City of Pittsburgh v. Pittsburgh Railways Company, Philadelphia Company et al. PA Public Service Commission Complaint No. C. 1571–1918.
Evening Public Ledger (Philadelphia). "Bankers Who Promoted Issue of Pittsburgh United Traction Form Protective Body." January 4, 1918.
———. "Bills Filed Against Big Traction Concern." February 14, 1918.
"50th Anniversary Philadelphia Company." *Public Service* 23, no. 5 (May 1934).
Fleming, George T. *History of Pittsburgh & Environs: From Prehistoric Days to the Beginning of the American Revolution.* Vol. 2. New York: American Historical Society, 1922.
Gazette Times. "Many Mergers Make Long Career of the Traction Company in This City." April 23, 1918.

————. "Mayor Will License Auto Owners for Bus Service During Strike." May 10, 1924.

————. "Railway Ends Receivership." December 31, 1925.

————. "Receivers for Trolley Lines Seem Assured." April 23, 1918.

————. "South Hills Tunnel Is Open to Walkers During Strike." May 10, 1924.

————. "Street Railway Receivership Ends." January 24, 1924.

————. "Traction Line Now Operated by Receivers." April 24, 1918.

————. "Trolleys Resume; Fares Stay Unchanged." May 13, 1924.

Philadelphia Company. Report of the Philadelphia Company to the Shareholders for the Nine Months Ended December 31, 1918. Pittsburgh, PA.

————. Report of the Philadelphia Company to the Shareholders for the Year Ended December 31, 1926; December 31, 1927; December 31, 1928; December 31, 1929; December 31, 1930; December 31, 1931; December 31, 1932; December 31, 1933; December 31, 1934; December 31, 1935; and December 31, 1938. Pittsburgh, PA.

————. 34th Annual Report of Philadelphia Companies to the Shareholders for the Year Ended March 31, 1918. Pittsburgh, PA.

Pittsburgh Post. "Readjustment of Traction Affairs Begun by Receivers Who Assume Full Control." April 24, 1918.

————. "S.L. Tone Put on Street Car Receivership; City to Ask Fare Increase." January 1, 1918.

————. "Street Car Men Strike Paralyzing Traction System Throughout City." May 15, 1924.

Pittsburg Press. "Fagan, Stewart and Callery Are New Receivers of Street Car Co." April 23, 1918.

————. "Former Judge Wasson, Made Special Master." August 27, 1921.

————. "George Is Named a Receiver for Street Car Co." December 18, 1918.

————. "Hundreds of Men Arrive to Man Cars." May 11, 1924.

————. "Seek to Force Philadelphia Company to Protect Bondholders." February 14, 1918.

————. "South Bound Tubes Open to Traffic, Victims Recover." May 11, 1924.

Pittsburgh Railways Company Records, 1872–1974, AIS.1974.29. Archives & Special Collections, University of Pittsburgh Library System Series I. Snow Report, 1872–1917.

————. Archives & Special Collections, University of Pittsburgh Library System Series I. Ford, Bacon and Davis underlying company maps [cartographic material]: taken from Engineer's valuation board report. Pittsburgh: Ford, Bacon & Davis, 1919.

Pittsburgh Transit Commissioner. Report of Transit Commissioner to the Honorable Mayor and the City Council of the City of Pittsburgh. 1917.

Thompson, A.W., president of the Philadelphia Company. *Pittsburgh Railways Problems*. Reprint from Chamber of Commerce "Pittsburgh First," an address to Pittsburgh Chamber of Commerce, March 7, 1922.

Tone, S.L., Pittsburgh Railways Company president. Annual Report to Board of Directors for 1918. April 1, 1918.

U.S. District Court, Western District of Pennsylvania. Equity Case File No. 201, May Term 1918. "American Brake Shoe and Foundry Co. et al v. Pittsburgh Railway Co." Petition of Pittsburgh Railways Co. March 16, 1922, American Brake Shoe Co and St. Louis Car Co.

———. Equity Case File No. 201, May Term 1918. "American Brake Shoe and Foundry Co. et al v. Pittsburgh Railway Co. City of Pittsburgh Intervener vs. Pittsburgh Railways Company Consolidated Traction Company Intervener." 1918.

———. Equity Case File No. 201, May Term 1918. "American Brake Shoe and Foundry Co. et al v. Pittsburgh Railway Co." City of Pittsburgh Petition to Intervene granted November 14, 1918.

———. Equity Case File No. 201, May Term 1918. "American Brake Shoe and Foundry Co. et al v. Pittsburgh Railway Co." Pittsburgh Railways Brief, 1923.

———. Equity Case File No. 201, May Term 1918. "American Brake Shoe and Foundry Co. et al v. Pittsburgh Railway Co." Receivers Petition Related to Accident Claims, July 7, 1919.

———. Equity Case File No. 201, May Term 1918. "American Brake Shoe and Foundry Co. et al v. Pittsburgh Railway Co." Petition of Pittsburgh Railways Co. March 16, 1922, American Brake Shoe Co. and St. Louis Car Co.

———. Equity Case File No. 201, May Term 1918. "American Brake Shoe and Foundry Co. et al v. Pittsburgh Railway Co." Response of receivers to proposed settlement, May 18, 1922.

———. Equity Case File No. 201, May Term 1918. "American Brake Shoe and Foundry Co. et al v. Pittsburgh Railway Co." Special Master H.G. Wasson opinion, March 31, 1923.

———. Equity Case File No. 201, May Term 1918. "American Brake Shoe and Foundry Co. et al v. Pittsburgh Railway Co." Civil judgements against Pittsburgh Railways prior to receivership.

Wall Street Journal. "Pittsburgh Railways: Federal Court Approves Lifting Receivership and Return of Road to Owners." January 25, 1924.

Victims, Rescuers and Caregivers

Allegheny County Coroner's Office Records, 1884–1976, AIS.1982.07. File 191802 (203–228). Archives & Special Collections, University of Pittsburgh Library System Subseries 1. Coroner Case Files 1887–1973.

Gazette Times, Pittsburg Dispatch, Pittsburg Press, Pittsburgh Chronicle Telegraph, Pittsburgh Gazette, Pittsburgh Post and *Pittsburgh Sun*. https://www.newspapers.com

Pittsburg Press, Pittsburgh Post, Pittsburgh Sun, Pittsburg Dispatch, Pittsburgh Chronicle Telegraph, Hilltop Record and *Gazette Times.* Carnegie Library of Pittsburgh, Pennsylvania Department. Newspaper microfilms.

University of Pittsburgh Library. "G.M. Hopkins & Co. 1916, Volume 6 (Revised 1922 and 1928)—Plat-book of the city of Pittsburgh: South Side and Southern Vicinity of Pittsburgh (East Half)." Historic Pittsburgh. https://historicpittsburgh.org/maps-hopkins/1916-volume-6-plat-book-pittsburgh-south-side-southern

University of Pittsburgh Library. "G.M. Hopkins & Co. 1917, Volume 7 (Revised 1928)—Plat-book of the city of Pittsburgh: South Side and Southern Vicinity of Pittsburgh (West Half)." Historic Pittsburgh. https://historicpittsburgh.org/maps-hopkins/1917-volume-7-plat-book-pittsburgh-south-side-southern

Internet sources

Ancestry (https://www.ancestry.com), Find-a-Grave (https://www.findagrave.com), Fold3 (https://www.fold3.com), Historic Pittsburgh (http://historicpittsburgh.org) were used to gather publicly accessible information from census, naturalization, immigration/emigration, birth, marriage, death and military records and city directories about individuals included in the chapters of this book, especially Victims, Rescuers and Caregivers.

Image Credits

Archives & Special Collections, University of Pittsburgh Library System, Pittsburgh City Photographer Collection: Mount Washington Street Car (715.162652B); Carrick Street Car (715.162652C); Carson and Smithfield (715.112489); Diamond Street (715.133629.CP) and South Portal of Mount Washington Tunnel, Pittsburgh Railways Co. (7429.0051.PR).

Library of Congress Prints and Photographs Division: Bauman, J.J. "Pittsburgh, Pennsylvania, View of Skyline." 1916. https://www.loc.gov/pictures/item/2018645172/; "Pittsburgh Soldier's Good-By." Circa 1915–circa 1920, George G. Bain Collection. https://www.loc.gov/item/2014702045/.

Record 0Group 10, Office of the Governor, Governor Robert P. Casey Proclamation (series #10,3). Courtesy of Pennsylvania Historical and Museum Commission. "10,000 Members." https://digitalarchives.powerlibrary.org/psa/islandora/object/psa%3Awwip_542. "Boys and Girls You Can Help Your Uncle Sam Win the War: Save Your Quarters, Buy War Savings Stamps." https://digitalarchives.powerlibrary.org/psa/islandora/object/psa%3Awwip_701.